SOULFUL

By

T.B. HUMAN

To order additional copies of this book, contact:

Lesley Halverson Australia +61 417722693

www.lesleyhalverson.com

DEDICATION

To My Readers,

My intention in sharing this very personal story with you is to
encourage you to find a little extra courage, and to cling on to hope
even when life seems to keep handing you lemons.

This is a true story. It tells of my own battle with depression and how
my sensitivity helped me cling precariously to the hope that one day
life would be better; and not only that, but that somehow I could
make a difference in this world.

To all my companions along the way … I honor you, and all that
you are and will become. Thank you for the experience.

Lesley Halverson.

CONTENTS

If you dare walk down the path today

You better not walk alone

If you dare seek healing on the path today

Beware of what beckons you on

For once the path of love and peace

Stripped bare and naked my bones

I screamed to God what have I done

God answered, 'keep going, the battles not yet won.'

Authorised Endorsements

Everyone's story is different, but in a way, the same. They're the same because everyone is either marching toward the truth or away from it. Those are the only two choices. But ultimately we all march toward the truth. It's just a choice of when. Lesley's journey is a march toward the truth, and where she can, she'll take fellow travelers with her as companions. I am but a fellow traveler and companion.

—Jenny Brassel,
author of *Secret Reflection—Trust in Dreams*

A compelling masterpiece on the drama of life, *Lesley* shares selflessly the heartbreaks and joys of one woman's dramatic life experience and the journey she must face to find true love. This is literally the PhD from *The Secret*, and provides the key for achieving the greatest life experience possible.

—Tracy Weslosky,
Entrepreneur & CEO, ProEdge Media Corp

Reading *Soulful*, for me, was like finding the key to a hidden treasure box. Nonfiction so raw and telling of the author's journey, it was as if I was walking with her. I could close my eyes and travel along on her adventures in the Bush and throughout her life. I found myself crying as I have felt her struggles too, realizing they paralleled my own life in many ways. I didn't want the book to end, but I couldn't put it down. Surely whomever this book finds, will know exactly why it came to rest in their hands.

—J. M. Dare,
author of *36 Sense*

When I read the book, *Soulful*, I smiled, I cried, and I remembered all those memories that you're triggered in my own life. All I can say is that I devoured it and came out wanting more; I need to know the rest of the journey.

— **Leanne Marie Roberts**

Food to nourish the Soul; this book reminded me in so many ways of my own journey. However, it's as though the writer, Lesley Halverson, has done what I (and probably many) have been too afraid to do. I was gifted with hearing and sensing spirit at an early age and have always had spiritual dreams. However, I have blocked a lot of it out due to fear. This book is a game-changer in the arena of spiritual self-discovery. Soul-blaringly honest, this raw account of one woman's journey to unveil her true purpose will engross your mind and spirit.

— **Kirsten Mc Lachlan**

Lesley shares her tender and relatable story of faith in seeking and seeing the truth and appreciating the contradicting harshness and beauty of life experience. I learnt a lot about Lesley and a lot more about myself. Her vulnerability is now my strength. She has put me at ease knowing I am not crazy, but mindfully alive. If *Soulful* doesn't open your heart you might want to consider a heart transplant.

— **Gipsy Grace**

There is so much I want to say. You can't imagine how many similarities there are in our lives, about a decade apart. I've assumed I'd write a book and have beginnings and notes poked in all sorts of places, but I think I can consider it done! I started reading that night and finished last night. I'm not a big reader; most I start don't finish and have never read a book in less than 24 hours before, totally enjoyed our story. Thank You!

— **Susie -Victoria**

PROLOGUE

This book is in fact my daughter's story; however, I felt the reader would benefit from understanding how our lives were all shaken to the core by choices and events which brought us to here. Looking back now, I often wonder if her life would have been different if we had not boarded that boat bound for Australia, a decision that would change all of our lives forever. How different would all of our lives have been? Would life have been easier? Would there have been so many hard lessons? At my age now, I still find I have so many unanswered questions. I decided, in order for the reader to fully comprehend the impact of family decisions upon my daughter, I would need to tell the story right from the beginning.

May 23rd 1956 was the day we stood on the deck of the migrant ship and watched England slip away into our past. My Jim and our four children were pressed close to me by the surrounding crowd. It was a strangely silent crowd, as one by one the hawsers dropped from the dock and the ribbon of water gradually widened between ship and shore. Almost reluctantly, the great bow turned to the open sea and then, like people released from a trance, came the last minute calls … 'Take care of yourself.' Voices echoed above the sounds of the engines, 'Don't forget to write. Goodbye …' 'Bye …'

The echoes faintly came back from the already tiny figures on the docks while the docks themselves dissolved from view into the fine spring mist.

The touch of a gentle hand upon my arm roused me from the numb ache that had held me motionless. Turning my head with an effort, I looked into my husband's sympathetic eyes, 'Come on, Love.' he murmured, giving my arm a gentle squeeze, 'Let's go and get settled, a long journey ahead.' Our ship dropped anchor on 24 June one month and one day after leaving England. The morning was fine and sunny and, as we were not going ashore until the afternoon, we finished packing and enjoyed a leisurely meal. When we went ashore at 2 pm, a light drizzle had begun to fall. By the time we were cleared by customs, the drizzle had turned to a steady downpour.

We shivered in our light summer clothing as we waited for the private bus that was to take us to the camp. I had packed our heavier clothing, thinking we would not need it. It was almost dark before the bus arrived and we were far too uncomfortable anyway to take an interest in the route we took. After half an hour's run, the bus came to a stop and the driver called out cheerfully, 'Here you are folks. Home sweet home!'

That is where our story began, a migrant's camp in a Sydney suburb. From there, we stepped into the unknown, trusting that God and fate would see us through. The precious 'three hundred pounds' (all we possessed) paid for the old truck, supplies, and the deposit on our farm land; or should I say, block of virgin bush. We were determined to make a better life. As we clung to each other, we clung also to the dream that somehow life would be better and things would work out. But that, in itself, is another story.

SOULFUL

Leaving England affected us all, but most of all Lesley. Being the youngest, she missed her older brother desperately; and having her whole world turned upside down, would leave her with gypsy feet from that day onwards. I am not surprised that the prediction made by a Gypsy woman in 1950 has come true. She said I would have another child, and this would be a very special child; for the blood and strength of queens would flow deep through her veins, and her heart and soul would carry the vision and wisdom of a great intuitive healer.

An excerpt from *The Last Sixpence* by Marjorie Williams

LESLEY SPEAKS ...

Everywhere people are searching, searching for a sense of safety and belonging. In spite of the fact we live on an abundant planet where there is more than enough to provide for everyone, there are far more that live in poverty and abuse than in plenty. Children go without food, mothers cry for sons and daughters lost in useless wars, and suffering continues. I question the purpose of this suffering; is it the only way our consciousness can be provoked to wake up? Is suffering the only way to shake us out of our complacency? I know there have been times on earth when our Indigenous ancestors lived in harmony with Mother Earth. But today, we have grown fat and lazy; people have become greedy, and take more than they need. Not only that, we have forgotten how to listen to the nature of our gut knowing. We have long been sleeping in a sleep so deep that if we do not soon awaken, we surely will destroy ourselves and this beautiful blue planet.

I am troubled by what is happening in the world today, I do not know how our lives and our earth are to be repaired; and yet, I feel the urge to share my story; to speak. This is not about spirituality, or religion, it is about humanity getting back in touch with its truth. It does not matter what form it takes, the important thing is we begin to listen to what we know is right. We must work together and find new ways of bringing community back into daily life, or we will fail as a civilization and it is that simple.

My intuition grows stronger with each passing day; I have been shown that it is the ultimate way to stay safe in this world. And yet, the fact that I am intuitive seems to conger all manner of fear and superstition in those around me. My intention with this story is to shed some light on the reality of the nature of life. For me this reality is about how we have reached a time when it is critical to connect all of humanity through the power of the heart. This is the only way to heal emotions and perceptions as a part of developing consciousness. And in time, it is the way that will change the tide and restore health to this small blue planet. Each of us must take on the challenge. And when finally we have healed enough of our own issues, we can make clearer choices; and in that, experience freedom from contaminated emotions and destructive patterns of behavior. The old ways must change. We must bid goodbye to the days of blame, hate, fear, and greed.

I came into this life with lifetimes of wisdom—held waiting like fairy dust, to be restored to me as I faced each trial, each initiation of character presented to me. I have seen the past. I have seen time and time again, me standing hand in hand with the man I loved, and I have watched as the world around me tore itself to shreds. And each time I vowed that, by God, it would not happen this time. During my life's journey, I opened Pandora's Box, moving into the spiritual and the psychic and by doing so, my life was shattered into a million pieces, and what was left was hope. In the long run, I walked away from it all; because it is not the answer. There is more...

As a child, I was happy and loved my life. And yet, being an English immigrant, I never felt like I fitted in with the other kids. I was the youngest child of seven, and my parents were lovely, good ordinary people. I was incredibly shy, so I loved to spend my time alone, being creative. I would draw and paint and make things out of scraps. I made puppets and clay pots from the red ochre clay I dug from a hole in the wall of the dam. I sewed all my own doll clothes from fabric scraps gathered when my mother sewed. I would sit my dolls up and tell them stories of my adventures in the bush, gathering stones, plants, feathers and other small treasures. I loved to sing, and often belted out the full chorus of Maria at the top of my voice while standing in the middle of our ten-acre block of land. I laugh now when I think of those innocent days, and wonder what the neighbors must have thought of this child singing so passionately to an audience of birds and wallabies. In childhood I had no fear—not of the Bush, or of the animals that lived there. I felt more comfortable with nature than with people; people actually scared me to death.

Some of the kids at school were just plain mean and nasty; I could never understand why they were just so horrible to each other. My parents didn't treat each other like that; they were always so kind, caring and loving to each other. I could never understand people who told lies, stole or were nice to your face and said bad things behind your back. My parents didn't have money; in fact they didn't own much at all, but we all had everything we needed right there in our tiny home. Mum and Dad were married for forty-five years when my dad passed away. Right up until then, they were still in love, and still walked down the street holding hands. That is how I always thought life should be, safe and happy.

Every single person has a story. The nuts and bolts, the heartaches and betrayals, the love, and the fearlessness are all factors which make us who we are. I have heard it said that the first six years of life form the subconscious patterns and initiate the development of our personalities. We then seem to spend a lifetime trying to overcome and release the misconceptions of a child's perspective.

When my mum and dad made the decision to emigrate to Australia, they thought they were doing the right thing to ensure our family had a better future. My parents had no doubts about their decision to move and they were willing to give up all the security they had in order to give us a better life. They were particularly worried about my brothers growing up in London with the street gangs and the lack of opportunities.

It must have been such a hard decision leaving everyone behind—my nan and my aunts, as well as all of our friends. The support was gone and there was no turning back. My big brother Rhys announced that he wasn't going to Australia. He was going to wait and, when he was old enough, head for Vancouver to join the air force. His decision broke my mum's heart, but he was of an age where she could do little about it. So decisions were made and plans to start again were put in place. Things were sold or given away, packing began; and before we knew it, we were on the boat heading for a whole new life.

I was never really meant to be born. Mum told me the story of how, when she was around the age of forty, my other sister Olwyn, who was only three months old, unexpectedly passed away. The grief was all too much. Mum dug a hole and buried the pram and baby things in the back yard. This was the old superstitious way of preventing pregnancy. Mum swore to God there would be no more children for her; the grief of losing two children in her lifetime was more than enough. Life went on as normal. There was some talk of the family emigrating to Australia but at that time my granddad was still alive, although very ill. In 1952 Mum noticed she was putting on a little weight, which was very unusual for her, as she was such a tiny woman. Time went past and she thought it was just the menopause taking its toll. However, a trip to the local doctor had her and my father shocked and amazed. Mum was over six months pregnant. Despite having made my appearance into the world rather unexpectedly, my dad always said I was the twinkle in his eye, and for sure he loved me with every inch of his great big heart and soul.

CHAPTER ONE

'Question everything—seek to understand greater meaning in all experiences.'

I woke with a jolt and a shake at the droning of the motors as the huge ship clanged to a shuddering stop. The grey gun metal walls carried the sound throughout every cabin; there was no escape. Sleep was shattered by the endless drone of the motors; no matter how tired you were, it still somehow seemed to be elusive. The grinding of chains as the anchor was dropped, and the bangs and clangs of the ship being tied at the dock were all just a little too much that day. We had been sailing for over six weeks with nothing but a rocking deck below our feet—nothing still, nothing quiet, and nothing familiar. I cried, wishing that I could wake from this nightmare and find myself tucked safely into my old bed in the upstairs front room of 36 Chorleywood Crescent, St Paul's Cray, back in Kent. Just in that moment my mother snatched up my hand and pulled me from the bunk where I had been sleeping, 'Come on, Sweetie, up you get, time to get dressed. We have to go find Dad and the boys.' Rubbing the sleep out of my eyes, I quickly saw the opportunity to escape by darting out from under my mother's grasp, out the door and down the hallway. I was free, with my sister racing after me, 'Lesley, come back here. Come back. You don't know where you're going!' Patricia yelled at the top of her voice, 'Dad isn't down there. You'll get lost. Come back!' And that is how it all began. We had arrived, and all I wanted was to get off that ship and head for home—London.

'Form a line here,' one of the deckhands roared, waving his hands dramatically as though directing traffic. People pushed and shoved, everyone was in a hurry to get off the boat, and no one noticed a little girl caught up in the stampede of legs and feet. I had no choice. I could still hear my sister's voice somewhere in the distance, 'Lesley where are you?' I was helpless as the swirl of people pushed me onwards in the queue, and I was scared. The tears began to fall, and the sobs just rocked my body as the people kept pushing. 'Daddy, I want my daddy,' I sobbed. And with that, just like a miracle, two big strong hands reached down and scooped me up. The next thing I knew, I was bouncing on my dad's shoulders. 'Come on, Blossom.' he said, 'what do you think you are doing out there?' A gentle hand steadied me so I wouldn't fall. I knew my dad would never let me fall, not ever.

On the docks, men struggled to shift the cargo and clear the passengers to the holding bay where everyone's papers would be processed. The sun was shining and although it was a pleasant day in the middle of winter in Australia, we found the day to be very taxing indeed. After that, my father wouldn't let me out of his sight but the other kids were old enough to know better than to wander far from Mum and Dad. The heady smell of coal smoke swirled around the dockside, as the steam trains pulled up at the platform. Finally, after hours of waiting, our family was bundled off to temporary accommodation in the migrants' camp a few miles away. Our family left England with the princely sum of 350 pound sterling. In the weeks to come, my parents would buy a truck, put a deposit on a block of land, buy the basic equipment to set up camp, and we'd all travel the 650 miles up to sunny Queensland. Our family was about to get a very fast and very big introduction to becoming homesteaders and farmers.

So I was only three years old when our family set sail to the strange new land of Australia and life was turned upside down. Looking back, I guess it was the shock of everything that triggered the awakening of that part of me which called upon something bigger than I could imagine at the time. For one thing, we no longer had a house to live in. Instead, it was replaced with a large canvas tent and camp beds. As well, the strange new life surrounded by the Australian bush was a very scary place at first. This was particularly so without my big brother Rhys to protect me. Night time was especially uncomfortable. I would reach down and pull the heavy blankets up around my ears and hold my breath, trying not to make a sound. I could see them—the visitors who came in the night—the glowing balls of light that hovered, watching, ever watching. Couldn't everyone see them? My canvas camp bed was no place to hide. Even the heavy blankets were no protection from the visitors' prying eyes. If I could get up the courage, I would flee to the safety of my mum and dad's bed to hear Dad's reassuring words, 'What's wrong, Blossom? It's only a bad dream. It's alright nothing's going to hurt you.' And he tucked the blankets in tight around me, giving me a quick kiss on the forehead.

My parents were intent on making a home for the family. Settling in the Queensland bush involved cutting down the timber to build our house and clearing the land to grow food. Their vision was that we would become self-sufficient. In theory it all sounded good, but in fact it was just plain hard work. Local Australian kids had houses and their parents had jobs, and they had toys and food and pretty dresses. Our family was reduced to accepting hand me downs. We wore plastic shoes and had no bath tub. Every day Mum would take us down to the creek, which was about a mile and a half down the dirt track, to make us take a bath in the clear, cold running water. I can still hear her voice, 'We may be poor, but that doesn't mean you have to be dirty. Now get scrubbing!'

The fact that I didn't feel I fitted in as a child probably was a real blessing in disguise. My mother said I was born curious, always wondering what was at the end of the garden, and always asking questions. There were always so many questions: What is at the end of the sky, Mum? Are we there yet, Mum? Can we go home now, Mum? What if we get lost, Mum? What happens when we die, Mum? How come? Why are people so mean, Mum? How come people go to church, Mum? I talk to God in the paddock, Mum! I must have driven her to distraction with all my questions.

I tended to play on my own, climbing trees and having wonderful adventures in the Queensland bush that I grew to love and understand. My mother gave up trying to keep a leash on me and finally surrendered to buying me a little fox terrier dog to keep me company on my wanderings. Tiny was a very protective dog. She knew the dangers of snakes and would warn us if one was near. She had caught and killed over fifty-one snakes in her lifetime that we knew of. So as long as Tiny was with me, Mum felt she had some measure of keeping me safe. My mother always said that if Tiny ever came home without me, then she knew I was in trouble and to come looking for me. Thankfully, that never happened.

Many things happened to me as a child and some things which should not have happened. I was only about 5 when sexual abuse began. It should still never have happened but it did, later my brother would deny it ever happened, but at the time, I was far too afraid to tell my mum or dad. I was bullied by nasty children who lived not far from us, and there were more nasty kids at school who simply picked on us because we were emigrants. My two older brothers had been enrolled in the primary school before me, and apparently been a bit of a hand full. So I was the last in our family to have to be taught by teachers who had suffered my older brothers' antics before me. They had branded me as 'one of those brats' and they were always eager to hand out punishment at any opportunity. Mr. Kruger's favorite weapon was a split ruler around the legs. For asking to go to the toilet I was made to stand in the corner for hours on end, and then had to suffer the humiliation of peeing my pants when my tiny bladder could not hold any more. School days were nothing but misery and abuse for me. Not only from other children but from teachers as well.

The harder I tried to learn, the more the ruler came down on my knuckles with Mr. Hayes screaming, 'What is that, a chooks mess!' Mr. Connor, he was my English teacher, and his trick was to make me sit on my left hand so I would not try to write with it. I was then humiliated, punished, and eventually sent out of the room because I would not stop crying. I have to add here, I was so quiet and shy, nothing like my brothers. School was a very cruel and torturous place back in 1959. Needless to say, I hated school and I found it so difficult to be stuck in a classroom day in and day out, let alone trying to make sense of words. The teachers thought I was just plain stubborn as I much preferred to sit and stare out the window. It wasn't until many years later that I was finally diagnosed with a

mild case of dyslexia, and so many things about those years made
sense.

I guess I was lucky in that my disadvantaged childhood turned
out to be an advantage in the long run, for already I had begun
learning how to make the glass always seem half full. My basic
instincts were fueled by the need to stay safe and keep myself out of
the way of the brown snakes and the black snakes which inhabited
the bush around our farm. I learned to listen to feel the energy of the
bush, and to know the warning signals, a bird life suddenly flying or
the thick sound of silence all were warning signs not to be ignored.
Our small plot of ten acres was carved out of the scrubland inch by
inch by my father's hands. The land had originally been Aboriginal
tribal land and had been given the Aboriginal name of Moodlu,
meaning hill of stone. We were only about five miles from the Glass
House Mountains. These were the sacred mountains of the Kabi-
Kabi Aboriginal tribe. A bora ring[1], was just one kilometer south of
the mountains, served as a place of initiation for young men. The
Glass House Mountains also have great cultural significance, as does
Moodlu, a sacred corroboree[2] ground.

---

[1] *Bora rings* are **mandala**-like formations found in south-east **Australia**. They
comprise circles of foot-hardened earth, surrounded by raised embankments. They
were generally constructed in pairs (although some sites have three), with a bigger
circle about 22 meters in diameter and a smaller one of about 14 meters. A *Bora* is
the name given to an **initiation** ceremony of **Indigenous Australians**, and to the site
on which the initiation is performed. At such a site, boys achieve the status of men.
The initiation ceremony differs from culture to culture. The ceremony, and the
process leading up to it, involves the learning of sacred songs, stories, dances, and
traditional lore.

[2] **A *corroboree*** is a ceremonial meeting of Australian Aboriginals. The name
Caboolture is derived from Kabi words, meaning 'place of the carpet snake'. Kabi is

Coming from England, we knew little about the Indigenous Australian people, but we were later told that the original people who lived on our land were Kabi-Kabi people. They were great environmentalists, living in harmony with the land. They harvested bush foods to eat; including freshwater mussels, oysters, fish, and some game animals. Being somewhat nomadic, they moved around the land to take best advantage of seasonally available produce. The big red hill up the top of our road was in fact the sacred corroboree ground where the Kabi-Kabi tribe met to hold ceremonies. Over the years, a gaping cut revealed where half of the mountain had been carved away to be used as rock for the highways. Now, only the memory of the Kabi-Kabi people remained, their physical presence had long gone from these lands.

Our closest neighbors were a family called the Parkers. They lived at the top of our road and had two children living at home, Kaleen and William. Mr. Parker, a tall severe- looking man who never seemed to smile, worked for the PMG (what us kids called the local post office). He was definitely a man of very few words. Mrs. Parker was a short, plump woman who always was as neat as a pin and wore her glasses perched on the end of her nose. She was always laughing, and she baked the most delicious cookies and cakes I have ever to this day tasted. Mrs. Deventer was Mrs. Parker's mother. She lived in a separate weatherboard house with amazingly high stumps in one corner of the land. Nana (Mrs. Deventer, as she was called), always appeared incredibly old, even when we first moved to the bushland farm. I had heard it said that when she first moved to

---

an Aboriginal tribe of this area.

Moodlu, the Aborigines were still there. The houses of white settlers were built high at that time so that they were protected from attacks by the Aboriginals. Thankfully, she survived. Mrs. Deventer was always so kind to us kids. There was always a cheery word and a glass of cordial and, if we were lucky, a scone with real fresh cream and some of her home-made jam. Her tiny, wizened frame moved swiftly from one task to the next. One couldn't help but be constantly amazed at her dexterity.

I remember the first time I met the Parkers. My mum had sent my brother Paul and me to buy some milk from old Mrs. Deventer. With a shiny sixpence and milk billycan in hand, we wandered up through the hot, dry bush. The cicadas were singing in the midday heat and the heat waves were rising on the road in front of us. We were barefoot and grubby from playing in the dirt while Mum chipped the weeds from around the newly planted crop of peas. We must have looked as if no one owned us, two scraggly English kids with sweat and dust smudged from head to foot and the bare essentials of clothes.

Mrs. Deventer's cows terrified me; I barely came up to their bellies. I was so small, but I recall that everyone was standing around laughing as my brother and I tried to negotiate the paddock with Blue Bell and Jess, the big guernsey cows, hot on our heels. Can you imagine it, two kids from London being chased across the yard by two huge guernseys? That paddock seemed so big; I never thought I would reach the gate alive. My little legs moved so fast; I thought for sure they would tangle in a knot and I would be trampled by the massive beast hot on my tail. 'Just keep coming. They won't hurt you,' Mrs. Deventer called out in her strong Cornish accent. 'Come on now, Blue Bell and Jess. Don't go giving those children such a fright. Away yea go cow, go on now!' Mrs. Deventer was wielding a piece of stick which was bigger than her, menacingly at the cows. She loved those old cows and just didn't want them coming in the house gate. 'They saw you carrying the billycan and thought you had a treat for them to eat, that's all,' she smiled a knowing smile as she ushered us through the old wooden gate and carefully replaced the wire hoop around the stump to keep it closed. Then she asked, 'Now you two, are yea all right? Come on now,' Mrs. Deventer reassured us, 'They won't hurt you.'

The cow paddock was about two acres of long grass. At one end there was the milking shed. At the other was the old house, perched high up on its incredible stumps. I remember I counted the steps once and there were over forty of them. My goodness, that house was so high off the ground! 'Come on then, you want some milk then? We have to go down to the dairy shed, just follow me. Those old cows won't hurt you,' she smiled. You could hear her chuckling, but she was trying to remain composed so as not to offend us. 'Haven't you ever seen cows before?' she asked.

'No, Mum,' my brother Paul answered with his broad cockney accent. 'We didn't have cows in London, only a milkman.' Mrs. Deventer could contain herself no longer and burst into laughter as she strode off across the long grass towards the old wooden milking shed. The shed was dark and smelt of cow dung, as all milking sheds do. I held my nose and watched where I stepped so as to try to avoid the recent wet pats of cow dung. I watched with curiosity as Mrs. Deventer went to a large metal milk can, lifted the lid, then reached for a large pouring jug and dipped it deep into the thick set of cream floating on the top of the milk. I had never seen milk like that, before coming to Australia. The cream would settle on the top of the milk to be inches thick and Mum would scoop it off so we could have it on our porridge, or she would make butter out of it. It was so nice and just plain yummy.

At the moment Mrs. Deventer poured the milk into our tin billycan, she turned towards the door and said, 'Hello, you two, I wondered how long it would take you to see we have company.' A face peered through the wooden slats and another 'round the doorway. 'Children, these are my grandchildren. Come on in here and mind your manners,' the old lady beckoned. Kaleen was a slim girl with milk-white skin covered with freckles, and the longest, reddest ponytail I had ever seen. Her hair was like spun copper; it glowed in the morning sunshine. Kaleen was about the same age as my brother Paul who, by the way, also had the most incredible red hair. Her little brother William was about my age, chubby, and happy. He eyed the situation, as though measuring us up to see if we were ok.

By now, the milk billycan was full and the lid was securely put back on. Mrs. Deventer turned and said, 'Now, would you all like a drink of cordial and a biscuit before you leave?' Of course, we just smiled. 'Yes, please,' everyone answered. Who could refuse a treat like that, fresh baked biscuits and cordial? What a luxury it was! Lately we had only had the bare essentials in our lives, and no jam. We were lucky to have dripping (beef fat) on a piece of bread.

That was where my story began, back in the days of innocence. It was a time when you could safely wander anywhere without worry or fear. Kaleen and William became best friends with us very quickly and soon we would be skipping up and down the dirt track three or four times a day, back and forth. The bush was our playground; it had miles and miles of thick gum trees and endless sunshine. There were so many strange things in this land. It was fascinating, even for a child four years of age. My adventures were amazing and soon became the focus of my life. I went where no one else had gone, I saw what other people didn't notice, I watched the bandicoots and the wallabies, I followed lizards and annoyed the heck out of the big anthills. It was summer, the days were hot, and the Queensland bush had a smell all its own. The heady smell of eucalyptus leaves warming in the midday sun and cicadas singing their deafening song left such a powerful impression on me. To this day, it is something that takes my mind right back to my childhood memories.

Life was hard but it was also very simple. The bush and I meshed in a way that is quite difficult to put into words. Who would ever have guessed that those days of innocence were to unfold to be the foundation of my spirituality and would open doorways never entered by any other white woman? Fifty-eight years later, I have found the courage to tell my story. It is one that some may not believe, but most will be able to relate to. Continuing on …

It wasn't long before we settled into the Australian way of life. The long, hot days were spent doing chores such as tending to the crops, carrying tins of water up from the creek, and chopping wood for the stove. My mother was a tiny little woman but she worked tirelessly to plant the crops and tend the paddocks that Dad had cleared. By now, my older sister Patricia had left home to go and work for the railway in the city. Helping Mum was left to Christopher, who was the strongest of us all. Being the youngest, I was largely left to my own devices. This gave me a great deal of time to myself and I soon found favorite magical places to explore, and felt the deep inner contentment that came with wandering in the bush.

My older brother and I teamed up with the Parker kids and the four of us would hang out together. I would usually trail behind

Paul, who was the same age as Kaleen, while William and I were best friends. We sort of looked out for each other in a weird and wonderful way. On weekends and holidays, the four of us would arrange to meet and plan our next adventure off into the bush. We would go on grand adventures to the river and anywhere our pushbikes would take us. The local dam, located beside the main road to Wamuran (a small country farming town a few miles away), was a favorite place for swimming. The dam was actually a hole that had been left to fill with water after the roadwork's built the main road. We had no idea what was in the bottom of it. The water was always brown and had a particular smell but, as kids feeling the summer heat, we really didn't care.

Kaleen and William were born in Moodlu, so they knew all the cool places to explore; like the old abandoned railway house and the quarry with its cliff face, loading platform, and tunnels. God knows how we didn't kill ourselves. We were children who knew no boundaries. The bush was our playground. One day we would be pirates; the next, cowboys and Indians. We were up trees, over paddocks, down the creek, and back home again. I think our mothers would have had a fit if they had known just how far our adventures had taken us and how dangerous they were.

One day, in the middle of the summer holidays, the four of us were sitting under the big mango tree at the bus stop in front of Mrs. Kola's house, when my brother Paul came up with an idea, 'Why don't we climb the face of the quarry? That would be fun.' We all just looked at him.

'Climb the face of the quarry? You have got to be kidding!' Kaleen retorted. 'You will kill yourself. Do you know how high that is?' My brother got that mischievous look, not really thinking anyone would take him up on the challenge. He was just trying to impress Kaleen with his bravery, which was more like stupidity, I thought.

'You do know that is sacred Aboriginal ground, don't you?' Kaleen firmly stated the facts. 'You shouldn't go up there. You know its bad luck to walk up there on the hill,' she continued. 'The Aboriginal spirit people watch that place. It used to be their land and all the tribes had ceremonies up there.' At that time, my brother Paul thought he was bulletproof and invincible. I remember him as a skinny kid with red hair, no shirt, and this great big knife in a leather shield strapped to his waist. What a sight! And he thought he was so cool—another James Dean!

He was out to prove to the world he was brave and definitely not afraid of some Aboriginal superstition. So off Paul set, and the three of us all followed—Kaleen first, then William, and me tagging along behind. The first challenge was the hill near the road. It was covered in lantana, a very spiky flowering bush that seemed to spread like a tangled web of vines over the countryside. Paul pulled out his knife and began hacking a path through the undergrowth; I think he thought he was some famous explorer. We all obediently followed. We were scratched and feeling sorry for ourselves but it wasn't long before we scrambled up the edge of the outside rim of the quarry. It seemed very high to me, and looking down into the quarry was somewhat frightening—I didn't like heights.

Looking back, I don't know what my brother must have been thinking. Mum would have killed him if she'd known he had gone there and taken me with him. It wasn't a safe place to be. The rock miners were off work for the weekend, so there would not be any blasting today, but still the huge cliff face of rainbow-colored shale loomed up out of the massive hole in the ground. 'Well, are you coming, or are you all scaredy cats?' Paul taunted as he headed off towards the downhill path to find his way to the quarry floor.

I began crying very loudly, 'I can't climb. That's too big!' Tears were streaming down my face and the thought of having to climb the face of the quarry was just about the most terrifying thing I could ever have imagined. 'Go on, sookie baby. You walk around and up the hill to the top. We will come and get you when we have made it up the face.' Paul just didn't care. He had it in his head he would climb the face of the quarry, and that was that!

I stood there, feeling very lost. My face was stained with dust and dirt from scrambling through the lantana bushes. Still sobbing, I watched as the three of them disappeared off into the distance down the hill into the quarry. I wanted to run after them, but I was so afraid. The rocks were sharp and jagged under my feet. I was scared to death. I looked up the hill that the quarry face was on. That wouldn't be so bad. It was rounded and covered in loose stones, but at least it wasn't a vertical cliff face. So off I climbed, almost on my hands and knees, or should I say hands and feet. I leaned over, gripping the rocks and sort of walking on all fours as I made my way up the hill towards the top. I was still crying and muttering to myself, that I was going to tell Mum when I got home. Paul would surely be in trouble for leaving me here. He was always in trouble for one thing or another (I don't know why, but he seemed to both love and hate living in Australia and rebelled at the harshness of life at every turn.). Off in the distance, I could see three tiny specks as they walked on the floor of the quarry. Paul was boldly leading the way, with Kaleen and William trailing behind him like a string of cattle, as they wandered towards the steep face of the cliff.

As I looked again to the top of the mountain of dirt and rocks before me, my hands and feet inched their way with caution, one tiny step after the other. It was ok; there was nowhere much to fall. I was well away from the cliff face and was working my way sort of around towards the top where Paul had told me to wait. As I climbed, I kept getting this peculiar tingling sensation, as though all my hair was standing on end. You know, that feeling you get when someone is watching you, but you can't see them. It gave me goosebumps. So through the dust, dirt, and tears, I began to sing to myself so I wouldn't be scared. I just had to get to the top as soon as I could and wait for the others.

The closer I climbed to the top of the red rock hill of stone, the stronger the presence became around me. I was sure someone was about to leap out and yell, 'Ha, ha, scared you!' So I just kept my head down and kept inching my way up the hill. About an hour later, I arrived at the top. It was a strange place. I could see where areas of stone had been cleared to make stone circles, and there was paint on some rocks. It looked like something you would see in a book. I found a spot with no sharp rocks that looked like a good place to sit. It was in the middle of one of the stone circles. The sun was hot. I was thirsty and feeling very, very tired. All I wanted was to go home; I didn't want to play this game anymore.

I don't know how long I sat there; it could have been hours as I must have dozed off to sleep. I don't think I was dreaming; it all seemed far too real. I felt a shadow cross over me, blocking the harsh sunlight from my face; and through squinting eyes, I looked up to see something I never could have dreamt. Looking down at me was the strangest looking man I had ever seen. He was tall and lean, and his skin was painted in white and red bands of ochre[3] paint. There were feathers bound to his ankles. His hair was the fuzziest I had ever seen, and his nose was so broad that it looked as if someone had squashed it right on his face. He was like an old grandfather and I think his smile was intended to reassure me that he meant me no harm. As he spoke to me in a language I didn't understand, he reached out his dark, bony hand and gently touched my forehead.

I watched as he squatted down on his haunches, steadying himself with a long stick that he held in one hand, decorated with paint and feathers. As he gently touched my face, he spoke words which I am sure were supposed to calm and reassure me. All that I could understand was that he kept saying the words *Apari-Orad, Apari-Orad*[4]. My eyes felt so heavy. Although I resisted closing them, I was so tired I just couldn't keep going. I felt a reassuring peace descend upon me and a deep sleep overtook my tired little body. Somewhere in the deep recesses of my mind, I heard the word W*uriupranili*. I didn't know what it meant but I instinctively felt the old man's eyes watching over me, looking into the depths of my soul. Looking back now, there was no fear, and it was a sense of an overwhelming feeling of peace and of being watched over and protected.

I drifted deeper and deeper into the most incredible dream sleep. It was as though I could feel myself travelling through time. My dream carried me to where I could hear children laughing and playing, and a dog barking. There were sounds so gentle—cicadas

---

[3] Ochre clay was used for making paint by the Aboriginal people. It comes in various colors of red, yellow and brown.

[4] **Apari-Orad** = Father Earth Apari—Aboriginal name meaning father. Orad—meaning earth.

singing a midday chorus that sounded like a million bumblebees fluttering their wings, and the tinkle of the creek running over polished river bed stones. It felt strangely familiar. The creek was just like the one behind the Kolas' farm down the hill from the quarry. I could smell the water and the heady scent of the trees lining its banks. Its gentle, rippling current and the shade of the trees were a soothing contrast to the heat of the day. I don't know how long I slept. It could have been a few minutes or an hour; I had no way of knowing. Lost in the dream, I joined the other children, never questioning that they were very different from me. It was as though I belonged—myself, the dream, and the dreaming.

'Can you see her?' I heard the voices echo from down the hill, and a voice echoed back, 'No, not yet. She must be here somewhere.' It was Kaylen's voice.

Then I heard my brother's voice fill with panic, 'Mum will kill me if anything happens to her!'

'There she is. Up there,' William called out, and soon the three musketeers scrambled up the hill towards where I was waiting. All were looking tired, and covered in red dirt from head to foot. It was time to go home. The sun was beginning to descend in the sky over the sacred hill, and our parents would be wondering just where on earth we had taken ourselves off to.

Now reunited, everyone was talking at once, and I gathered from the conversation that Paul was the only one to attempt to climb the quarry face, ultimately to find it was too scary even for him. Apparently, they all had given up on the plan and decided to backtrack the way they had come and then climb the hill from the sloping side, just like I had done. I tried to tell them of the Aboriginal man who had spoken to me, but they all laughed.

'Aborigines haven't lived here for over fifty years now. They moved out long ago. You dreamt it, there's no one here.' My brother ruffled my hair with his hand, 'Come on, Sis. Let's get you home.' He gave me a hug, and I think my brother quickly realized he had been a little bit mean to me. Or was it, he didn't want me to tell Mum and Dad because he would have got a flogging? I wonder . . .

Although I didn't know it, the events of the day on the quarry hill were to change my destiny. From that day onwards, I never felt alone when I ventured off into the bush around our farm. I felt the protective eyes of Apari-Orad watching over me every step of the way. Occasionally, I would catch sight of him watching from a distance. He was often seen in the shade of a tree with his thin, lean frame balanced standing on one leg, the other foot braced upon his knee. He perched like a statue with a spear in his hand, his ochre painted face and body glistening in the midday sunlight; and the mass of thick, dark curls bouncing in the breeze. Sometimes he would simply nod to me, acknowledging I had seen him; then he would silently slip away, melting into the background, as though he were never there. No one else saw him in those days, and I never thought to question that fact. All I knew was that he was my friend and life was good.

Time was passing and I was growing fast. Dad had built our first house and we now had a well, so water was close by. The land was growing crops and day by day we settled more and more into this new way of life. I still had a lot of time to myself because I was still too young to work the heavy farm machinery, so I would just wander off to watch the birds and pick wildflowers. Strange as it may seem, I felt as though I was becoming a part of the land that surrounded my home. I knew every inch of our property and loved the solitude of nature. I felt like the land spoke to me and taught me about the nature of what lived there. I was becoming aware of all that was living around me—the birds, the kangaroos, and predators like the king brown snake. A deep awareness of life now accompanied me just as constantly as my Aboriginal guardian. It was as though a sixth sense was the only way to relate to an ever-changing canvas of color developing around me.

Days passed with me sitting high in the branches of my favorite paper bark tree, just watching and listening, learning the sounds and echoes, and feeling that this was where I belonged. It was as though I were seeing how alive everything was and learning to feel the sense of movement, the seasons, the animals, and the earth's energies as they played and roamed in the natural bush. When you're alone in the Australian bush, something very special happens.

I have no doubt it was my guardian who subtly taught me how to feel the energy of the land, the animals, and the plants. As I watched and listened, sitting so still, just breathing in and out, I found that if I could be still enough, a strange thing would happen. I would become one with my environment, or part of something other than myself. I became the wallaby. My energy blended with his to the point where there was no separation between us. I could feel the power of his strong body and I could sense the subtleties of his keen awareness—the heightened sense of sound and the smells which guided and protected him. It was as though I could hear or know what an animal's next move would be.

Without knowing it, I was learning the skill of empathy—the sensory skill of using the senses to connect to other living things. The smell of the gum trees on a hot summer's day—that heady scent of eucalyptus filling the air—gave me the feeling that if I stood still long enough, I could just vanish into something far bigger than myself.

Many years later, I learnt about an ancient practice used by Tibetan Lamas in their training. A young student would be sent out to contemplate something in nature. His task was to become one with the tree or the mountain, or whatever it was that the Guru Rinpoche (beloved Master) had set for his focus. The only way to achieve this connection is to be very still and open to the quiet subtle energies. Lamas generally meditate to learn this skill but I was doing this at a very early age without even knowing that was what was happening. Every day was a lesson, every day was a wonderful adventure into the natural world of things; and every day, my instincts sharpened. The 'school of life', Mum would call it, 'the best school anyone could attend'.

Days were flying past quickly and soon turned into years, each one merging with the next. Life was very difficult for my mother and father, as Dad was in a terrible accident and broke his back and neck when a tree fell on his earth-moving equipment. He was in the hospital for months and there was no compensation or any type of government support or help for injured workers.

I never forget going to see my dad in hospital. We travelled on the train into the city, and there was my dad, plastered from waist to neck. It was so scary. For weeks, he was in hospital, so we had to survive any way we could. I can remember Mum working in the fields, trying to grow a few vegetables. She had to swallow her pride and ask the local green grocer to give us credit. We kids used to walk the highway, looking for soft-drink bottles to take back to the shop for a refund of 3p. Every penny counted; every penny went to food and basics. If we didn't have the money, we went without food—it was that simple.

Payments on the farm were falling behind, but Mum and Dad

protected us from all of that as much as they could. There was little food to eat or treats to be had. Mum baked bread of simple flour and water and we had dripping smeared on it for a treat if we were lucky. We grew vegetables and there was always a meal on the table, a simple stew of beef and vegetables. Mum could make a tasty meal from practically nothing. We were always hungry and no one noticed my mother getting thinner and thinner until she weighed only about 4 stone. Something had to give and yet I can never, ever remember seeing her cry or complain. Life went on as best it could. My brother Paul was now about fifteen and hated school so, after discussions, it was decided that he would go off to work. It wasn't long before he found a position as a farm hand, mending fences and shooting kangaroos on a property out in west Queensland. I was left on the farm with Mum, and Dad came home from hospital just before Easter in 1959. He took a long time to recover from his injuries, and life was hard.

Locals came to the rescue whenever they could. Someone gave us a few scraggy chickens and we had eggs. Someone else gave us a goat and we had milk. A dozen apples here, or a pail of milk there— people were very kind. One man in particular turned out to be a great friend. I only remember him as Burt. Burt would turn up with money or groceries just because he felt so. He was a great support to my mother and father, who by now had run out of money and out of luck.

My guardian was not to be my only spirit visitor. I came to know four regular guardians from the spirit world and over the days to come, I would be introduced to my teachers one by one. The lady in black was elegant and stately with her hair piled high upon her head. Her role was to teach me to handle challenges with strength and dignity. Aligning with my Aboriginal guardian was to teach me to be aware and to learn to use my senses to feel and interpret my surroundings. The Lord Jesus Christ with his red golden hair and beard, glowing white and blue robes, and the most amazing blue eyes I have ever seen, was a fisher of men. He would reach deep into my heart, bringing alignment to the Christ principles for living. He also provided me with strength, and faith to meet the challenges which were to come. The fourth was a very unusual man I have come to know as one of the Moorish people of Europe. He was very tall with dark skin and he wore robes, along with a turban-like headpiece. Profoundly versed in mystical practices, I now know that he is one of the Sons of Light, the original Knights Templar. His role was to help me learn the secret teachings of the ancient Creators, or Sons of Light. On many occasions he has scared the living daylights out of my house guests by standing at the foot of their beds and watching over them during holiday visits. As you see, each guardian has a direct purpose. Each one has a quality he/she instills into my life. And each has earned his or her place in history during their physical incarnation. It's funny when I think back. I never, for one moment, thought other people didn't see these spirit guardians too. It never crossed my mind that I was the only one in our family, except for my mother, to know that they were there at all. These spirit visitors were a part of my everyday life during my childhood on the farm.

The night was cold; we had experienced a very early winter. Often in the mornings, the ice crackled on the grass as we made your sprint down the backyard to the outhouse. But the evening was pleasant, sitting in front of the warm fire, with the Tilley lamp sending off a lovely yellow glow to fill the space around the table. Mum was sitting reading her book and Dad was just sitting back humming a song. The light reflected the lines on his face and I thought I must be a very lucky person indeed to have such a feeling of love all around me. 'Come on Blossom, off to bed now. Time all good girls were tucked in bed.' My dad scooped me up in his big strong arms, tickling me at the same time just to make me squirm. With a swinging motion he spun me through the air as though I were a plane. I squealed with joy and then was dumped down into my kapok mattress. It felt so good, so safe, and so snugly.

'Dad, it's cold. Can I have your coat on, please?' I begged. 'Please, Dad, can I?' I knew that the coat smelled of my dad and it made me feel so protected and safe. The heaviness of it was like a guard against the outside world.

'All right then,' he smiled. (His eyes were blue and they sparkled in the light of the lantern.) 'I'll go get it for you, but you can have another blanket instead, you know. You sure you want the old coat?'

'Yes, Daddy, please. I love your big black coat.' With that, and one giant swoosh, the huge black trench coat landed on the bed. And then, my dad was carefully and gently pulling it up under my chin, pretending to tuck me in so tight I couldn't move. All I could do was giggle and squirm. It was a regular game, one filled with love and security.

'Night night, sleep tight. God bless,' he ruffled my hair as he stepped away. Soon Mum was there. Her tiny frame was checking to see that I was all tucked in and ready for sleep. 'Night, Love,' she said as she leaned forward to place a kiss on my forehead. 'See you in the morning, bright and early for school.' And with that, she swiftly left the room, leaving me to the darkness, the warmth of the coat, and the sleep that was fast descending upon me.

I very quickly fell into a deep, peaceful sleep. I don't know how long I had been asleep when something woke me with a start. The house was dark and very quiet, as my brothers and my parents were sound asleep. Yet I had an eerie feeling that I was not alone. Someone was watching me, I could feel it. I had goosebumps running all over me. My eyes had not yet adjusted to the darkness of my tiny room. I tugged at Dad's big black coat, pulling it up so it was nearly covering my face and I could just peek out to try to see what was there. Over the next few minutes as my eyes got used to the darkened room, I began seeing the shapes of the furniture and the doorway going into Mum and Dad's room. I couldn't believe my eyes as a shape began to form at the end of my bed. From it, a glowing light began to emerge and standing within this radiant glow was the most beautiful looking man I had ever seen. His white robes shone with light so bright, and his hair looked like soft spun gold falling gently down over his shoulders. His eyes were soft bright blue and he was smiling down at me, just smiling. I remember thinking, I must have been bad if he is here. I must have been really bad! Panic filled my head, and my heart raced at a hundred miles an hour. I grabbed for Dad's big heavy coat and pulled it right up over my head. I can still remember how scared I was. I had never seen anything like him. He was glowing, and people don't glow!

I still remember what happened as if it were yesterday. I pulled the covers back down, thinking, when I look back he will be gone … When I look back, he will be gone. But he wasn't. Instead, he was smiling 'so big' and almost laughing; he looked quite amused at my attempt to regain some form of composure. So I just looked at him and he said, 'Little one, it's all right. I am here to watch over you always.' The mysterious man in the glowing white robes seemed to be thinking, as he stopped what he was saying for a moment and looked to see if I understood. 'No matter what happens, you will be safe always. It is time for you to begin remembering why you were born and what you have come to this life to do.' With that, he held out his hand towards me and it was as though the air became alive! 'Life will be a challenge for you,' he continued, 'but you are strong. You must question all things, do not give up. It is your challenge and yours alone to find the truth.' I couldn't have imagined such a thing could happen. My family was not religious and we didn't speak of visions or apparitions or the like. We were just ordinary people, or so I thought. The Lord had come to me, and all I could ask was, 'Why me?'

CHAPTER TWO

'A natural flow.'

Like many of my friends, my early teenage years were plagued with insecurity. I was growing into a young woman all too fast, my body faster than my wisdom. Hard times continued for my mother and father. My brothers had now left home and I was the only child to help on the farm. Bills piled up after Dad's accident and the sad day came when my parents had to auction everything we owned in an attempt to pay our debts.

We moved from the farm when I was about eleven years old and went to live on North Stradbroke Island. Life had changed, and there was nothing I could do about it but go with the flow. Dad managed to get a job working as a plant operator for Consolidated Rutile. I was enrolled in high school and the three of us lived in an old ten-foot caravan which had a bath tub built into a lift-up panel hidden in the floor. Once again I slept in the tent, but on a bed this time. Life continued on its journey and there was regular money, but still little luxury for my parents and myself.

By my early teens, I already had my first job and my first

boyfriend. My mind was on anything other than the spirit visitors from my childhood. My mother was a very outspoken person and I had inherited her mannerisms. I often spoke openly about what I thought, and had no idea that I was already beginning to use my senses to know if people were being honest or telling lies. Diplomacy was not something I was good at and my tendency to blurt things out resulted in my big mouth putting people offside. My life was full of school, swimming, and walking on the beach. I made some good friends, worked at the local cafe at night and on weekends, and I was growing up way too fast. I wasn't really comfortable around boys, as I was never sure of how to react. I found myself saying and doing stupid things, often ending up feeling embarrassed at my own naivety. Teenage years can be very complicated. I didn't drink or smoke like many of my friends and, according to gossip, I was in fact the last virgin in the group of girls my age. 'Live for today' was the attitude of the day. The Beach Boys sang out their songs on the local radio station and the girls dreamed of love and happiness. I trusted my senses for the most part, but I was still at the age where my emotions and hormones were playing havoc with my head space.

It was around the time of my fourteenth birthday when I was still going to high school, that my carefree attitude towards life was about to be changed. In the evenings, I used to work at the local cafe where I helped out with preparing meals for the miners. The cafe consisted of a front area, and at the back was a large dining room or mess hall where the sand miners could come to have their meals. I worked for a man named Rick Star who was an ex-boxer. He and his wife Sheila were nice people and always looked out for my welfare, because I was still at school and a little too trusting and naive about the world. Mum and Dad agreed to my working evenings, and of course on weekends, so that I could gain the practical experience and skills needed to gain full-time employment when I did leave school.

My mother and father had lived through many hard times. The war in England and growing up in Greenwich were among the worst. People who had a good attitude towards work were always in a better position, so in our family we were encouraged to have a good work ethic and it was expected that we would be financially independent by the time we left school. Each of us kids had our first paying job by the age of about twelve. Learning how to work for a boss was no small thing in life. My dad used to say, 'You must always give 110 per cent, and always do the best you can possibly do. That is what our family did—we worked hard, were honest, and could be trusted in any job role.'

One night I was walking home from work with a young man who worked for the sand mines. He was tall and handsome and in my mind he was someone I thought I could trust. After all, I had seen him at the mess hall every day for months and he had always been so nice to me. What I didn't see that night, was that accepting that innocent walk home would change my life forever. I had unknowingly placed myself at risk, simply by trusting the wrong person. I guess the reader can imagine what happened next. Grant asked me if I wanted to come to his room and talk for a while. He told me that his friend George and my friend Carol would be there. So I thought there was no harm in this, or danger—and against my better instincts, I agreed.

My innocence was about to be stolen, my confidence shattered, and the secret guilt was about to start accumulating. I hid what had happened from my parents. I felt dirty, guilty, and ashamed. The thing that had happened was something that could never be taken back, never fixed, and never given to that one love in my life out there somewhere waiting for me. The decision not to tell anyone, I thought was the right one at the time, but who knows? All I decided was that I would keep on as though nothing had occurred. The shame of the whole situation overwhelmed me, and I was somehow convinced that no one would understand that what had happened was not my fault. I finally told my mother about the incident when she was eighty-two. She was astounded that I had kept such a terrible thing to myself all those years.

By the time my fifteenth birthday had rolled around, my natural beauty was blossoming. I was in love with life, and a handsome boy as well. Every aspect of my creative talents for painting and art had begun to flourish. A tiny camera was by now my constant companion. Photos and artwork filled my room, and visions of working as an artist filled my head. My family could not afford to send me to art school so I was encouraged to apply for a scholarship. To my surprise, I won! My thoughts were filled with the dream of going to college and having the opportunity to become a commercial artist. For a precious moment, life seemed to be offering me the golden hand of opportunity.

Add to this mix my social life, which was very simple and yet, at the same time, so complicated. I liked two different boys who were best friends; one was English and one was Australian. Over the year I fell deeply in love with the younger man and the passion of love blossomed between us. I can still recall the first time I ever saw him. It was as though an electric shock ran through me. That feeling of love at first sight was not just a myth after all. Handsome, with dark brown eyes and a broad English accent, he was charming and fun and always fooling about. He used to blush and was also very shy, which I found to be attractive. We would often go driving to the beach, or swimming in the pool; and his friend, the Australian boy, would be there. It's funny how two people can be so different and yet be so much alike. The Australian boy, or should I say man, oozed pure sex appeal, he had a vibe that was like honey to a bee. We often teased each other about silly things; I suppose it was our way of keeping each other at arm's length because of my relationship with his friend. I found his cool charm and his self confidence very seductive. This man was a James Dean bad boy; he was handsome and cool as a cucumber. He was the type who is always in control, always quiet and strong. He drove a big flashy car with a big silver eagle across the bonnet. It was really strange but there was a different vibe with this man. There was a knowing, a gut feeling that I had known him before. It was as though there was a connection between us that pulled me towards him in a different way.

One night, while walking home from work, I was passing the men's barracks when I looked over under the streetlight and there was my boyfriend's car. There were two people in the front seat, clearly making out. A stab of pain filled my heart, and tears ran down my face as I ran the rest of the way home. I was so angry and I couldn't stop crying. How could he do this to me! I would teach him a lesson he wouldn't forget. The following Saturday, I accepted a ride home from work with his friend, the Australian boy whose name was Henry. And before either of us realized what was happening, we were in each other's arms and the fire of desire was raging between us. He was twenty-four years old and I was fifteen. The law was against us. The odds were against us. But desire crushed any rational thinking into dust, and we became lovers in the back seat of that Ford Falcon on a cold and wintery night in March. I thought I was grown up; at least my body looked grown up. Miniskirts and beehive hair were the fashion of the day and I was about to graduate junior high and go to college.

Up until this time, my life had been simple. I spent my days on the beach, an endless ribbon of clean, white sand. The surfing was amazing on the deep waves of the blue Pacific Ocean. Up until this time, my life had also been safe. Life was very different back in the sixties and early seventies. Parents made the decisions for you, and you did as you were told and treated anyone older than yourself with absolute respect. My life was about to change and, even though I had played a part, I would have no control over what was about to happen to me and the next twenty-five years of my life. My life was about to be torn apart and tossed into chaos. A new life was about to come into this world; a little girl would become my saving grace, my sanity, my soul mate. I thought I was all grown up. The Beach Boys played on the radio, singing 'Good Vibrations', and the Beetles sang out 'Love Me Do'. I loved music and knew every word of every song. The stories of hippies in the parks filled the airways and the Vietnam War captured everyone's attention. It was truly a time of peace, love, and moonbeams. Surfing at the point, sunshine, and falling in love were on the agenda. Looking back, oh … I was so dreadfully naïve. And so, the price for love would be that the moment I surrendered to desire, a new young, precious life was beginning to blossom inside of me.

I never told my parents I was pregnant. I didn't even realize it myself, to tell you the truth, because I still had my period; but only a few spots, rather than the grand slam flood I was used to. The fact that I was pregnant unfolded in a bizarre way, just as so many things have in my life.

My father's grandmother was a Romanoff Gypsy from Ireland. As many people know, Gypsies are renowned for their clairvoyant or psychic abilities, and all of my father's family was no exception to the rule. My nana was psychic, my aunties were psychic; and believe it or not, my father was also incredibly psychic, especially when it came to anything involving his daughters.

When my older sister Patricia had her children, my father had morning sickness while she had none. He knew each time she went into labor. My mother was quite amused when he rolled around on the floor in agony as Patricia gave birth to each of her sons (in different years). It was quite a joke at work when Dad would start throwing up first thing in the morning, and when questioned, he would simply say he was pregnant again. The fact my sister lived miles away made no difference, Dad would just know. It was June 1968 and the morning ritual of throwing up had begun once more. Phone calls were made but when the answer came from my sister that she definitely was not pregnant, the focus turned towards me. I will never forget the look of utter despair on my father's face as he walked into the room, 'It's you, isn't it? You're bloody pregnant!' I didn't know what to say. I guessed he was right. I didn't really know. I had no idea about such things; I had never even held a baby, let alone know anything about how not to get pregnant. Dad refused to speak to me for weeks, and that broke my heart; but in fact, I must have broken his.

My mother and father talked in private. This whole situation had to be kept hidden. Family in England were not to be told; after all, it was far too shameful. My parents considered their options of what to do and the ultimatum was issued—I could either go and live with my Aunt Nancy in Sydney and have the baby given up for adoption; or, I could marry the father. Poor Henry, he had not only my father to deal with, but the local police were knocking on his door, threatening to have him charged with 'carnal knowledge with a minor'.

Discussions were had between my Mum and Dad, and Henry; and a plan was hatched. I of course had no say. We would leave Stradbroke Island and go to Gladstone, where Henry was sure he could find work. There, we would wait out the time until I turned sixteen. At that time, we could legally marry and then we could carry on with life as man and wife. In those days, society viewed an unmarried mother who kept her baby as the worst kind of person. It was felt that her morals would contaminate the child and that the shame would simply be too much for a family to carry. So in the flash of an eye, my future was snatched out of my control, as plans were made for me to be married a week after my sixteenth birthday.

The wedding day should have been an indication of what life was about to become. My husband-to-be had 158 dollars to his name. I had about 26 dollars from my part-time job. The few months passed, and I became ill with a kidney problem. I didn't know how sick I was and the doctors never mentioned the danger to me, or that it might affect my unborn child. I cried a lot in those months. Apart from being unwell, I was so lonely and scared. My parents were ashamed of me, and the life I had wanted for myself had just been torn away, gone in the flash of an eye. Henry and I did the best we could. We clung on to each other, waited for the day we could get married, and hid out as if we were criminals. I was under the age of consent, which meant that my husband-to-be could go to jail for getting me pregnant. It was a dreadful strain.

The wedding day finally arrived. Henry's brother was to be the best man. His parents and family had driven up from New South Wales for the big day. We all met and then drove into the city. It was about 11 am when the traffic lights in front of us suddenly turned red. The breaks were slammed on and the next thing I remember was the sound of smashing metal. Henry's brother had just driven his car right into the back of our car! A horn was honking and there were people running. Here I was, six months pregnant and big as a house. My future mother-in-law was covered in blood from gashes caused by her hitting the console between the seats of the car. Henry and I were in total shock, thinking we were not even going to make it to our own wedding. Our car was just dented; the back was smashed but it was still drivable. Eric's car however, was a write-off. The radiator had burst and steam was flying up in the air. The steering had been damaged and the front wheels turned sideways. That was how hard he had hit our car. Thankfully though, everyone was out. We all huddled together on the side of the busy intersection whilst a plan was made. First, we had to get to our own wedding. And then, we had to get Eric's car off the road and to a garage. What a mess!

Finally, at 2 pm we stood in front of the marriage celebrant at City Hall. The stress of the day had been too much and, as the marriage celebrant began saying the vows, I began to laugh. It was only nerves, but he didn't see it that way. 'Young lady, it seems you think this is all a little funny. Well, I can assure you it is not. The vows of marriage are a very serious thing and not to be taken lightly.' He peered over his glasses at me, looking me up and down, as though I were some piece of trash that he found distasteful.

'I'm sorry, it's been a long day. I know it's a serious thing.' I struggled to suppress a bout of hysterical laughter, as he continued.

'Who gives this woman to this man?' My father sadly looked at me and stepped forward.

'I do.' It was the saddest day of his life, I am sure. He struggled not to cry and looked at me with such a look of despair that my heart felt as if it was breaking into a million pieces.

And so I became a wife. Sadly, from that time on, it was as though my life took a turn in a direction I had no control over. Life became a matter of existing, when it should have been about living. The battle was not just for me. It was now one of a mother and child's struggles to survive. The pain and confusion increased with every passing day. Sometimes, being responsible and grown up at sixteen was a little more than I could bear. By twenty-one, we had three wonderful children and I had a husband who spent most of his time either at work or with his mates. Anything to do with fishing or hunting and he was there. I guess he didn't like having a needy wife and, in those days I must admit, I was totally dependent upon him for everything. We lived in isolated places mostly, so it was miles to the next neighbor, even further to go to town. I guess I was just plain lonely. Children fill a space, but there are times when you just need someone grown up to sit and talk to, and have a laugh with. My spirit visitors were very absent during those years. I guess I just had to get on with life and the day-to-day running of a household by my own efforts. Looking after family sure kept me busy and very, very tired.

We continued to move from job to job, going where the work was. I worked as a nurse for some time at Kempsey District Hospital. Wages were basic but we didn't complain. Henry had work driving a milk truck and we eventually bought our first home (fully furnished) for the handsome sum of 500 dollars. But it wasn't long before I became very depressed and lonely. I was just plain homesick, I think. So we sold the house and bought our first caravan. That was our first big mistake, for that little old house could have set us up for life if we had stayed. Now, like a tortoise, our home was on our back. And so, freedom and the world were ours. Somehow it always seemed like an adventure going from one place to another. Our travels had taken us from Stradbroke, to Gladstone, on to Kempsey, back to Stradbroke, back down to Kempsey, and then all the way to Western Australia to the mining camp at Jurien Bay. While on Stradbroke in 1974, Queensland had its worst floods in over a hundred years. At the time, we owned a small caravan and lived there with our two and a half children (I was pregnant with my son at the time). The rain poured down and these poor folk were living in a tent opposite us. The rain was torrential, the winds cyclonic. So we reached out a hand of friendship and opened up our tiny home to the very wet and tired family across the way. Rose and her husband Lee stayed friends with us from that day on. And as it turned out, everywhere we moved, they moved; or vice versa. I had finally found someone who I felt a strong genuine friendship with and before long, Rose and I became inseparable. Rose and Lee became our traveling buddies. One family would travel ahead and then call back saying, 'There's work here'. The other would then follow. A friendship formed that has lasted a lifetime; Rose and I are still best friends to this day. Western Australia was hot and windy, I hated it. I had never seen so many blow flies and maggots in my life, and the flies made life unbearable. Around that time, Henry's father took ill and died suddenly. So the decision was easy; only a year on, we packed the car and trailer and headed back to Kempsey, then up the coast once more towards home on North Stradbroke Island.

There was no work on Stradbroke at that time but Lee had called Henry, saying that they were hiring up at Maryborough for the Frazer Island sand mines. So once more, off we trekked with three kids, a dog, and a caravan. Our time in Maryborough was short; the government closed down the mining and once more we were left with no job and not much money.

But we did have a few memories to take with us. We had met a few people because of the work there and one lady named Margaret really tried to become my friend. She was so into the psychic that she found my abilities fascinating. I had been having a lot of pain with my back, related to a fall many years before. Too many years of farm work and heavy lifting had taken their toll. Margaret kept pushing me to go and see a man she had heard of. He was a psychic who lived in town. This may sound funny, but I did not believe in psychics at that time. Yes, I had abilities. And yes, I saw spirit. And yes, I felt life had a purpose and we were all here for a reason. But I did not believe in seeing psychics to have them tell you things about your future! Margaret kept on and finally I agreed to go and see this man who I thought had to be a crook or a sham.

Margaret took me to his house on the day. I recall walking in and this man with dark hair and a beard looked quite normal as he sat behind a desk and reached out a welcoming hand to me. 'Please sit, my name is Victor,' he said. 'I was told you would come.' And I thought, Oh yeh, for sure. My doubting mind was running on fast forward. 'You have a destiny which is bigger than you can ever imagine,' he paused while looking intently at me. 'But first you have things you must finish with your own life, obligations which you must fulfill,' he smiled reassuringly. I am sure he could clearly see I was terrified. 'You have three children?' (It was more of a question than a statement.) I nodded. 'You will raise two more children, but they are not your birth children,' he said with a strong confidence in his voice.

I shook my head. 'No, no more children for me. My husband has had a vasectomy,' I smiled. 'I don't want more kids.'

'Ah, it is not for you to say,' he continued, 'It is already written. One of these children is a very special child. And that child shall become the one who inherits your legacy.' By now, I thought the man quite mad. Legacy? What legacy? 'You do not know it yet, but your life is going to change greatly. You will become another person.' He looked at me very seriously, 'I am seeing an ancient book. You know, the ones with incredibly intricate writing, and embossed with color and images like the old biblical scripts. You wrote this book in times past, in another life, and in another century. You will bring that ancient knowledge back in a new form. I see you will help thousands of people with whatever it is you will do.' I just smiled. Yep, I have heard it all now. The little girl from the bush is going to do something important. Yep, I can hardly read and write, but apparently I am going to help the world.

'You are very close to your father and he loves you very much. You have seen what other people never see—the Masters in spirit, is this not true?' I nodded, looking bewildered. 'You were born with a special purpose. You chose to come and have this hard life to pay off your karma, your debts.' He was fiddling with a pencil between his fingers. 'Everything will begin when you live in the old green house. That is where your change will begin.'

'I don't know a green house,' I mumbled.

'You will know it, and when you are there, things will start to happen for you. You must trust because it is going to be something in the end, you could not have ever imagined. The money will come as you need it. Your husband will die from something that comes from the sea.' I stared at him in disbelief. 'You will marry a second time and be very happy.' He looked deeply at me, 'You have a problem with your back.' (It was a statement rather than an

47

observation.)

'Yes, I do actually,' I answered, feeling surprised.

'Will you let me heal it? You could end up in a wheelchair if it is not attended to.' Well, I had nothing to lose, so I agreed.

Victor moved around the table and knelt on the floor beside me, 'Could you please turn your back towards me?' I shuffled around on the chair so my back faced him. 'I will not touch you, but you will feel the energy from my healing. Is that alright?' I just nodded. I had never had anything like this done to me before and I had no idea what it involved. As he moved his hands, there was the strangest feeling in my spine and back. It felt as though something was being dragged and moved. It was as though a big magnet was being pushed over my back, and it was a bunch of iron filings being rearranged by the magnet. That is the only way I can describe the feeling. 'There, that is fixed. It may cause problems again when you are older, but it will not cripple you now.' Victor went on to explain more about my life and my past. I just sat there with my mouth open. How could anyone have these powers! It defied all that I had ever known. He said I had been born before and I had been very powerful in many lifetimes. In some of those lifetimes I fell into greed or lack of compassion for those in my charge. He laughed, 'I bet you find this lifetime hard, without your servants and money.' Damn, he was right. I always felt I had been born into the wrong life. 'This life is to teach you humility, my dear. When you learn that with all your heart, then magic will happen. Just wait and see.'

I left that little house on the side of the Mary River that day, feeling stunned. I walked out to the car where Margaret was waiting and hopped in. Just as I sat down, I passed out cold. 'Lesley, are you alright? Lesley, wake up!' Margaret was shaking my shoulder. I felt so awful; it was like I had been somewhere else and just stepped back through a doorway to now. I tried to regain my composure but I cried and I cried. I could not even explain what on earth had happened. Poor Margaret didn't know what to do, 'Come on, let's get you home and get a cup of tea into you, then you can tell me all about it.' I never did tell her what had happened. How could I? It was the strangest experience of my life. My world changed that day—there were more questions than answers. I had had my first introduction to someone of my own kind and I had no idea what to do about it.

A week later, we moved from Maryborough. Caravan packed and kids all fighting in the back seat, we headed for Mount Morgan where my mum and dad now lived. Dad had retired, and he and Mum spent much of their time camping and fossicking for gemstones of all descriptions. They had the passion for it; it gave them a hobby and provided an interest they could share. As we pulled our caravan into the yard, the kids ran to see their nana and pop. My parents really loved my children. They had forgiven and forgotten the past. Henry got along well with my family; he really tried in those days. Mum didn't like how he treated me, but she accepted him. I guess, in his whole life, he had never learnt to be kind and gentle. After a few days, Dad suggested we all take a trip out to the Sapphire mines at Rubyvale. We could camp and have some fun digging for gemstones. Who knows, we might even find a big one. So life moved forward again. I counted once, and we moved twenty-nine times in twenty years. I guess we were seeing Australia and doing what other people only ever dreamt of doing. Money was tight but we had a few dollars from holiday pay and there would always be that next job out there somewhere. A good machine operator like Henry could always find work, and sure enough he did—in the gem fields.

Life living on a gem mine was sure different—generators for electricity, and bore water for showers, and a coil of black pipe on top of the pump shed to warm the water. Life was good. During the day, when the older kids were at school, I would take my son in the truck with some mining gear and head for the bush. Once again I was back where I felt at home; only this time, I was digging holes and washing gem dirt, always looking for that next flash of blue or yellow sapphire. It was hard work and yet it was fun, and I loved it! The excitement of never knowing what was hidden deep in the earth, those precious blue black rocks soon became the focus of our daily life. I could tell so many stories of those days of endless sunshine, and even when it rained it became a chance to find a fortune right on your doorstep. The whole family would put on gumboots and raincoats and just head out to spend the day walking in the rain, 'Specking,' as it was called. We didn't have to do anything other than walk along the road or tracks or paddocks, eyes to the ground looking for that special little glint of gemstones. I always seemed lucky, finding several huge blue sapphires just lying on the ground, waiting for me to find them.

Days passed, and we met many of the locals. Henry had been working for one of the long-time miners so he had learned a great deal about mining in a very short time. We became friends with a couple who lived in Sapphire and before we knew it, we had bought a sapphire mine of our own.

The mine consisted of a ten-acre plot, wash plant, front-end loader, and enough mining dirt to get us going. We thought this was 'it'. We could have a good life now. We worked hard, pulled together, and staked a dozen or so claims for future work. We were eking out a living. Of course things were always going wrong. The wash plant would break; a bearing here, a belt there—that was life running a mining plant. During this time, Henry was becoming very distant and withdrawn; he began drinking more heavily. I guess he was worried and didn't know how to tell me. The pressure was on all of us at that time. We had little to no money and there was heavy equipment to run and pay for, but we survived. I became good friends with a woman I will call Eve for the sake of this story, and Eve introduced me to the world of swingers to which she belonged. I had never thought of having an affair, but it seemed that is what women on the gem fields did to pass the time. So before I knew it, I had been drawn in, naive and insecure to the other world of lusty passion.

He was handsome, charming and even well mannered; I never expected to do this, or to fall in love that's for sure. A miner himself, Graham had done this sort of thing before, he knew the boundaries, and played the game. Secret rendezvous in town, afternoons of unbridled passion restored joy to my life for just a fleeting second. I knew it was wrong, but I was lonely and empty and all I wanted was for that very feeling to go away and never ever come back into my life. I couldn't fix my marriage, and yet I wanted it to be what I had with Graham, I felt hopelessly torn.

Mining was a hard life; money was always short, except when you had a good run of dirt. Mostly we were lucky to get three dollar yard dirt, but once in a while we hit pay dirt, and yard count came up to ten, and even if we were really lucky Twenty dollars a yard, when it was mined.

Every now and then, there would be an exceptionally large sapphire to pull us out of the down-slide, but life for the most part was really hard. Henry was working 24 hours a day, grabbing sleep where he could, and drinking the rest of the time. He didn't talk, he didn't laugh, and he just did his own thing. I felt so lonely that I didn't know what to do about it. In my way of thinking, I guess I wanted a husband who would love me. The words of the psychic were still echoing in my head. I didn't want Henry to die. The thought ate at me a little more every day. I wanted to run away; maybe if I did Henry wouldn't have to die. The seeds of destruction were planted and I had no idea of just how devastating it would all become.

CHAPTER THREE

'In every moment, there are choices.'

The day I died and left my body began with all the normal things which accompany any major surgery–carry bag packed and kids sorted. Mum was looking after them while I would be in hospital. The doctor said I could be in hospital for up to ten days, depending on how well the surgery went and the results of the pathology afterwards. Cervical cancer is an insidious thing; hopefully they had picked it up early enough.

The only difference between me and other patients that day was the fact that I knew, I just knew I was going to die! Henry said I was being silly, but I told him I just knew something was wrong and I had this deep sense, something beyond rational thought, that I should not have the surgery. I tried to tell the nurse who gave me the prep medication, but she just gave me the 'bloody stupid woman' look. Her expression was enough to make me shut up and just go ahead with it, even though my gut feeling was so strong not to. The nurse helped me onto the large gurney table and I was wheeled through the corridors, down to the bottom floor where there were two operating theatres. I recall that very large lights hung overhead, and it was cold, so cold. The walls were of blue-grey cement, and everything smelt of disinfectant.

I was asked to put my arm out and it was strapped firmly onto a board, so the assistant could begin fitting a needle into the back of my hand. This was not how it was supposed to be. I felt so confused. What were my options? I didn't feel I had any, so the surgery went ahead at 9.45 am at a tiny hospital in the outback of Central Queensland. I do remember the needle being put in my hand and the injection being administered. The warm fluid began to flow into, and up my arm. 'Relax now, be over in no time,' the doctor patted my shoulder, as I felt the world falling away and my grip on control slipping. I remember thinking: I'm going to die now. I have no choice, it's all too late. Who will take care of my children?

My children were ten, six, and four at the time of my being diagnosed with cervical cancer. I was just twenty-six years old and had been married for nearly eleven years at the time. The anesthetic began to take effect. Soon, my head began to spin and I felt myself sinking deeper and deeper into the blackness and the nothingness that engulfed me. No one stopped to consider that I might be allergic to the anesthetic. After all, I had never had surgery before, except for my eye when I was six years old; but that was done with chloroform, something quite different.

What about my children? That is the last thought I remember having after that hot flush of anesthetic took hold. I don't know what amount of time passed; it must have been quite some time, maybe an hour or more. Suddenly, I felt a jolt. It was like a string being pulled out of the top of my head. The next thing I knew, I was floating. Awareness flooded into my consciousness. I felt free. I recall thinking clearly; this must be what it was like to be dead. I must be dead! I felt weightless and very odd. Below me was a thin, dark-haired woman lying on the table in a room full of people in blue. There were lots of lights and stainless steel tables and gadgets. At first I wondered, who on earth this woman was. Who was she? Then reality hit like a bolt of lightning, and in a flash I realized that woman was me. At that very moment the room exploded into a flurry of activity of nurses, doctors, beeping machines, and confusion. Someone yelled, 'We're losing her. Come on Lesley. Not yet, come on!'

My spirit, my soul essence, felt as though it was being drawn upwards through the thick black nothingness. I felt a warm sticky thickness in the air, but still I was compelled to keep going upwards towards the light off in the distance. The white light was hypnotic. I could not tell if it was coming towards me, or I was going towards it; I just kept moving upwards. Then, right in front of me, in the middle of the nothingness, was my ever-present guardian, my Aboriginal friend from childhood, the man who watched over me— Apari-Orad! I had not thought of him in years; and yet, here he was standing solidly in my path. 'Go back. You must go back. It is not your time!' he called out. As he spoke, he waved his arms in a motion to make me go back—back to my body, back to my life. But this calling to keep going upwards was stronger—stronger than his words, stronger than my need to hang onto my body. Like a moth to a flame I kept on moving upwards and onwards to what … I had no idea. I kept catching glimpses of people's silhouettes in the darkness. There were faces and full figures washing in and out, as I followed the white light to the point where it began to envelop me, embrace me, and fulfill me. I was home, that is all I knew. I stood in my soul's full power that day. Love encircled me, embraced me, empowered me, and welcomed me!

Wherever I was, it was so bright. It was just like being caught in a heavy, thick, white fog on the brightest of sunny days. The light of love was the whiteness which encircled me. There were colors too: the green, so vivid and the blue, so crystal clear. I had never seen colors so pure. On a hill in front of me there was a big perfectly-shaped tree. Three people stood under it. One was a woman in black, the second was a man in a flannel checked shirt, and the third was an extremely tall, thin man with dark skin. I knew them, but from where? It was surreal, magnetic, and so reassuring. As I took a step forward, my eyes were blinded for a moment with gold and blue light. As I strained to see past the brightness, I could not believe my eyes at who I saw. There, standing right in front of me, waiting with arms outstretched, was the Lord Jesus Christ! I was home! The feeling of love is something no words can ever describe, the feeling of absolute love! That experience was something so profound that I still carry the knowing of what happened—the sense of being loved beyond comprehension. The fullness of being totally loved was to be etched forever into my brain with such intensity that I could never forget it. I know that this physical world has no experience to compare with it. That day, I stood wrapped in the arms of Jesus. And one day, when it is time, I have no doubt … I know he will welcome me home once more.

His words were strong and gentle as he spoke these exact words: 'Child, why have you come home? It is not your time.'

'Please don't make me go back. It's just too hard. It hurts too much.' I sobbed.

'You know you have free will,' Jesus continued, 'but you must go back and finish what you have chosen to do. One day you will do as I do, in my name. Many small things in your life will change more than you could ever imagine, trust that you are loved. I know your journey is hard; remember, I am always with you.' But the burning question was - 'What had I been born to do?'

In a flash, I was jolted back into my body and could feel the pain of the surgery. The physical pain was incredible, I was so hot. Machines beeped, and oxygen flowed through the mask strapped to my face, as I tried to drag it away. Two nurses were present, one each side of my bed. One was slapping my face gently, 'Come on Lesley, wake up. Lesley, wake up! What is your name? What day is it? Where are you?' Questions were being fired at me one after the other. I guess it was to try to assess if I had any brain damage. My reflexes were checked, my vitals were checked, my surgical wound was checked. Ouch! Apparently, I had sixty-two metal staples up my middle. I felt as though I was on fire and my head swam with the memory of what had just occurred. 'You gave the doctors a bit of a fright Lesley. You're one lucky girl, do you know that?' one nurse remarked. 'We nearly lost you. Glad you decided to stay for a while longer. Those kids of yours would sure have missed their mum.'

The tears rolled down my cheeks. Did that really happen? Did I go all the way to heaven? I felt such confusion. If the Lord said I had to come back, well then, I must have something very important to do! With that thought, my mind began to slip away as the nurse administered the pain meds. And once again, I felt myself falling into a long, deep dreamless sleep.

I could not speak to anyone about what happened that day. The very thought of the intensity of that love and knowing that I was completely loved, would bring me to tears of relief. I recall his presence, his peace, and his gentleness as his arms closed around me, embracing me with a purity of energy I have not experienced again, even to this day. The bizarre thing about it all is, I was absolutely shocked that the Lord saw fit to open his arms to me. I am not a religious person and in fact, I never really believed there was a heaven before that day. The energy of being in heaven is something I will never forget. It is beyond what we can feel in life. It is so all encompassing. If words can ever explain, it is the essence of 'pure unconditional love'.

That near-death experience was to be the turning point in my life. I don't mean that it was when I began to actively change. However, it was the point when my reality was shattered. From that point onwards, I had to consider that there just might be more to life. From then on, new questions began entering my mind. Each challenging thought brought with it a shift in perception, which affected not only my thinking, but also the choices I would make in my future life.

After my near-death experience, I felt even more alone in the physical world. I was confused and afraid in a world where I really didn't feel I belonged. I didn't know how to finish what I was born to do; I didn't know what it was. I didn't know how to find the answer, or to understand why I had experienced this wake up call. In the late 1970s, near-death experiences were not openly discussed. No one ever mentioned being spoken to by Jesus, and if they did, they were thought of as being a tad crazy! For me, the choice was to either open myself up to psychiatric evaluation, or just keep quiet about the whole thing, and try to figure it out for myself. So, I chose to keep my mouth shut and just stumble on, doing the best I could to find some peace and sanity in the midst of the chaos. If I had still lived in England, I probably would have had a very different journey. My aunts, I have since found out, were all very interested in spirituality;

they often went to spiritual gatherings and spoke with mediums (people who speak to those who have died). I had no idea the family was spiritual in any way.

Turning all of my attention to my work was, as always, my answer. Gem mining was hard work. What we focused on in our mine was the precious gemstone, the sapphire. Centuries ago when the earth was forming, volcanic action heated minerals in combinations which ultimately created many forms of gemstones. As volcanoes erupted, gravel was spewed into rivers or into layers upon the earth. Over time, centuries in fact, these layers were buried with mud, sediment, and vegetation. Sapphires are not just blue as many people think; they also come in green, yellow, white, purple, and party-colored. Sapphires are heavy. So, when processed through a wash plant or a jigger, they sink with the ironstone to the bottom of the ripples in the shaker. They have coldness and a luster about them, and at times look like broken glass or lava rock. If in doubt, we would put the stone under our tongue to test it. A sapphire would be cold and heavy; a piece of glass or rock would be warm and have no weight. I loved this life; every day was an adventure. Every day, you just could hit the jackpot and find 'the big one'. People had found incredible stones in the past, and anything was possible. You just never knew what fate had lined up in front of you. Gem mining was in my blood and in my heart, and became part of my life. I felt as though every gem I found was a representation of the wisdom I was gathering about life, love, and my heart consciousness.

Life was hard, but it was good. Our relationship was actually very happy during the early years of living and working in the mine. Although our mine was not big, we were able to process 150 yards of dirt a day on a good day. Sometimes the dirt averaged 5 dollars a yard, other times 35 dollars. Every day I learnt more about grading sapphire, where to find sapphire, and how to make sure the plant worked to its best and the sapphires didn't get washed down the chute into the dam. When the ground produced good stone, it was exciting. It does get into your blood and is like, as people say, an addiction. There was always that element of excitement, so much pleasure to be had out of tiny pieces of stone. Often, we had stone and no buyers. This made it so the few buyers who passed through, often only paid poor prices for the gemstones. That is how the life of a miner goes; always at the mercy of the market, the weather, and the quality of the ground you worked. Other times, there would be a flood of buyers, and then the competition made the prices higher. As long as we had food on the table and the bills were paid, we were happy.

My husband and I took it in turns working in the plant. Henry taught me to drive the front-end loader and the truck. I couldn't fix things if they broke, but I could pull my weight when it came to day-to-day operations. We would have the dirt carted in, and then spread it onto the drying fields where the dirt had to be absolutely powder dry before it could be put through the shaker. From the shaker, it fell into what was called a tumbler. Here, large stones were extracted and the sand fell to the floor. The gravel would slide down a shoot to the water-fed pulsation tray which shook up and down. It was a type of sluice box and, if we were lucky, the sapphires were extracted. I went to work for another miner for awhile to learn about gemstones—how to grade them, how to tell the quality, and how to judge what they were worth. It was a dirty, hot job sitting out in the middle of the yard for hours with buckets of gravel, and then tipping that gravel onto a table to have the sapphires extracted. Every few days, we would either have a buyer come to our home to bid on our stone or we would take the stones to a local buyer who would haggle over paying what the stones were worth. Our income was not big, we barely made ends meet, but we were happy for the first time in a long time. Unfortunately, it wasn't to last long. We all knew what was coming, the whispers were out. The Australian Government was about to blow apart the futures of dozens of miners, and only the strong and the very small would survive. As the pressures mounted, once again, Henry and I began pulling apart rather than pulling together to get through the bad times ahead. It was 1978 and all gem buyers had just been banned from entering Australia to purchase gemstones from Central Queensland miners. We had stone but, at the end of the day, it was of no use. Our mining operation ground to a slow trickle as we desperately tried to pay our leases, buy fuel and feed our family. The pressure was just too much, we began to argue and bicker. I was so angry and I have to admit now, I was a hell of a person to live with. I blamed Henry for everything but in reality, it was no one's fault. I had everything I ever wanted, but I thought I had nothing and wanted more. I had not grown up, and I was emotionally dependent. Self absorbed, immature, and confused by the events at hand, I needed space; and I needed to work out quite a few things about myself and my life. I just wanted to run away, and Henry felt he had failed us. When you want a relationship to end, without knowing it, you begin to do bizarre things to self destruct. I don't know why I did what I did, it all seems so long ago now, and so unimportant. I could have made very different choices if I had been able to see the destruction I caused in my wake.

The near-death experience had rattled me to the core and I was faced with a host of questions, most of which I just didn't seem to be able to find the answers to. The spiritual questions kept niggling at me too … Why was I born? Was there really a life after death? How could I find out what I needed to do? Why was I more sensitive than those people around me? How could I turn my unfortunate life around? How could I be healthy and happy? I felt like Alice in Wonderland. You know, I had fallen down the rabbit hole. And like Alice, the only way to get sense out of the situation was to go deeper into the rabbit hole and pray I came out the other side.

Along with all of those feelings, I began to feel grief-stricken and had no idea why. Finally, on Sunday, just before Christmas 1978 I had a feeling I just couldn't shake. I told Henry I was going to the post office to phone Mum. Something was wrong, I just knew it. The phone rang and my mother answered, 'Mum, is everything alright?' I asked.

'Love, Dad collapsed, they have taken him to hospital. How did you know? (I think my mother was crying, although she tried to hide it.) I didn't know how I could let you know. It happened just an hour ago. I'm so glad you called.' Mum reassured me that they thought it was just a kidney stone and that Dad would be home soon. Mum didn't want me to travel to Mount Morgan. It was a three and a half hour drive and the kids needed to go to school. As well, the little one was still a handful at home. However, soon my Dad was home and everyone kept saying he was fine, but a sense of panic still filled me from my head to my toes.

Inevitably, in mid-January, Dad collapsed again. This time I traveled to Mount Morgan Hospital and sat and waited in the hallway while they operated on him. I will never forget that feeling. I knew as soon as I saw the doctor walking down the hall towards me. I felt as though I was sinking in the deepest well of mud and grief. I felt as though my heart had become a piece of lead and struggled to beat. My father was dying and I knew. I went cold and numb. I heard the words and I just felt darkness. My mother crumbled into tears as the doctor informed us, 'I am so sorry, we can do nothing; the cancer has spread too far. He might have a month and we will do everything we can to keep him as pain-free as possible.' The doctor quietly went on his way, leaving our tiny family in a crumpled pile of tears and grief. Mum and Dad had been married forty-five years that Christmas, all Mum knew was life with Dad, nothing else.

I felt as though I was caught up in a hurricane of thoughts which possessed me, stealing what little happiness was left inside of me. I still felt extremely restless and unhappy. I would go so far as to say that I felt almost tragic within myself. Countless hours were spent wondering what to do. I worked harder and harder so I would not have to feel the pain and confusion, or think about the experience. It took only six weeks from diagnosis to death; in that time, the cancer had reduced my dad from a sixteen stone ball of muscle to a seven stone skeleton. I thank God he did not linger. My much loved father and my best friend passed away at 5.24 am on the 19th February 1979.

I was at home that morning and I knew the exact moment in time that my father had passed. I knew he would pay me a visit, and sure enough, goosebumps from head to toe, and there he was. Dad had come in spirit to say goodbye, and tell me he loved me. Dad told me not to cry, that he would always be with me, and he would look after me. As I watched, it was like looking through a void to another place. I saw an old cobbled street with street lamps, and my dad was walking away with the kitten I had bought him at his heels. He turned and said, 'Love, I am taking Thai Mai with me. She would only miss me if she stayed.' About twenty minutes later, my phone rang. It was my mum, telling me that Dad had passed away at 5.24

am.

In the evening of that same day, about 5.30 pm, the phone rang again. It was Mum, and she was so upset. 'You're not going to believe this. Thai Mai is dead! A dog got into the backyard and killed her. I can't believe I have lost both of them in one day,' she sobbed. Life would never be the same, not ever again. Suddenly I felt so alone. Dad had been my best friend, my soul mate, the one who always listened, and the one who was always there to pick me up when I fell. His death tore deeply into my soul, leaving a gaping hole that nothing could ever fill.

Chapter Four

'Live by your conscience.'

My best friend was gone, and for years to come the deep loss and unhappiness would consume me even more. No matter what I did, or how hard I tried, life just didn't seem to work. I was depressed, and wanted some knight in shining amour to come and take me away from all this. At home, the more I tried, the more everyone expected; the more I gave of myself, the more they wanted. I felt as though I was losing all sense of myself. I no longer had a life which was an expression of me. I lived for everyone else and tried to keep them happy. Deep inside, I just knew there had to be another way to live in the world. There had to be a way that people felt fulfilled and happy. Being the perfect mother and wife did not fill the hunger and the emptiness. Life just continued to be miserable. Something was missing, and I just had to find it.

I tried to find the answers by creating relationships with other men, something I am not proud of, that's for sure. I was a beautiful woman and men were eager to please me. My marriage was difficult and all I wanted was for the pain to go away. The need to feel loved is a powerful force; if having affection from some other man did that for me, I felt that was what I had to do to survive. I knew it was wrong, but I was so lonely and lost. There were no answers, only questions. I felt as though I was fighting for my soul and in thinking back, I probably was. There was just so much happening, I was totally out of my depth, and there was no one to offer me guidance or advice.

At the time that my dad passed away, Henry and I still lived in Central Queensland, working our small sapphire mine. It was a hard life, but I loved the bush and felt very much a part of the land. Business was so hard. This was around the time that the Australian government had placed an embargo on buyers coming into the country to buy the precious stones, and we had no money to buy food for our children. The life we had chosen, and the business we had been working a hundred hours a week, were being ripped apart by circumstances totally out of our control; and there was nothing we could do about any of it.

I began to learn much more about Henry than I ever thought possible. As a child, he had experienced a very tough and hard upbringing. Apparently, it was nothing for him to be tied to the clothes hoist in order to keep him where his mother wanted him. She was not a loving woman or, to my eyes, she never expressed love in the normal ways. Hard as nails! But again, I guess that is how people were in the early days; this is how they survived the harshness of life. Henry was also a no nonsense person. He was not comfortable with affection as such and constantly pushed me away as though things like that should only happen in the bedroom. Over time, his nature became harsher and more controlling. I felt so lost and hurt by the death of my father, the grief was consuming me. Our business was disintegrating, the debts were piling up, and our relationship was drowning in a sea of anger and frustration.

We were two people coming from such different family environments, trying to make life work. But actually, we had no common ground to hold us together except for sexual attraction and a commitment to our marriage vows. I longed for the sensation of being loved. Nothing filled that void but the love of my children, and I loved them back with such a protective passion—like a lioness watching over her cubs. My marriage was on rocky ground. Henry had begun drinking every day, and working longer and longer. We fought, we argued, we blamed each other for our misery, and I kept trying to escape. The years kept rolling out in front of us while three beautiful children were all that held us together in a web of joy and misery.

In the end, I couldn't take it any more (the pressure and the drinking) so I ran. I just had to get away from the anger, the arguments and the tears. The stress was making me ill, and all I wanted was just a feeling of safety and some peace. So once again, my mother came to my rescue by paying for our plane tickets; graciously, she took me to live with her for a while.

I soon found a job working as a cleaner in a motel complex. It wasn't much, but it would feed us, and with the added social security for the children, we would get by. There were no luxuries, or even a car to get us about, but it didn't matter. To get to work, I walked the four miles there and back every day. My mother looked after the children when they were not at school and life did evolve into some well-earned peace. There was one thing that troubled me though. I had left my son with my husband, hoping it would keep him sober; but I deeply regretted that decision. I missed my son so much my heart hurt, and I wished I had not let him stay with his father. After all, he was only three years old.

Time passed, I had been separated from Henry for six months, and I have to say most of the arguments had faded into the distance. My children were my focus, and somehow I was going to make life work. I didn't know it at the time, but the business Henry and I had worked so hard to build was all gone; nothing was left. Henry just walked away, leaving everything behind for any of the locals to pillage; and what was left, to the debt collectors. My leaving broke his spirit I guess, and then everything just became too much for him. The life on the gem fields held nothing for him anymore. The sapphire market was in a bad recession and so, he just walked away, leaving everything—our caravan, our furniture, even our personal possessions—he just left everything. He packed a bag for himself and my son, hopped in the car, and drove away never looking back. I had no idea Henry had left the gem fields; or for that matter, that he was living just down the road with his brother.

It was a Saturday morning. I had not long walked home from work and was still in my uniform when the phone rang. The voice sounded familiar, but I didn't suspect it would be Henry playing a trick on me. The man claimed to be my husband's brother, Mel. He said there was some news and he needed to speak to me. He asked if we could meet. I had an uneasy feeling as I listened but I ignored my gut feeling. I told Mum what was happening and she just said the usual, 'Be careful.' I left the girls with Mum and off I went to the park just down the road to wait for Mel. I stood there feeling really nervous when, at that moment, a brown panel van pulled up right next to me. There at the window of the old car was the smiling face of my little boy. His eyes were so blue and his smile so big. What could I do? My heart felt as if it was breaking into a million pieces. I opened the door and he flew into my arms. I hugged him as if there were no tomorrow.

Henry sat watching, eyes cold as steel, 'Get in the car woman,' he said with the usual anger in his voice. A part of me was glad to see him, but the other part of my heart sank when I noticed the loaded rifle across his knees pointing at the floor of the car. 'You get in the car now and come with me or I'll kill your kids one at a time in front of you, and then I'll kill you!' His words cut into my heart like a knife. I felt I had no choice. I knew what he was capable of. I had to go back to him as his wife if I wanted my children to live. Henry drove me home and I had to pretend nothing was wrong. I was shaking and inside me a voice was screaming. I made my excuses to Mum, never telling her what had actually happened. We packed our bags and drove away in the old Falcon Sedan. I felt that I had let my mum down—I had left her abandoned in a flat she could not afford on her own. I just couldn't tell her the whole story. She would have confronted Henry and then there would have been hell to pay. Mostly, I didn't want anyone getting hurt and that is the honest truth of it all. So, once again I played the loving wife, smiled, and pretended I lived in a perfect world.

All of those events happened in one short year—my dad passing, my separation from Henry, and our reunion. The year 1980 was such a traumatic year, I am sure that my spirit left me for a while. I was numb and dead to living. But my children were the most precious thing in my life, and I would do anything to keep them alive and see them grow into independent capable people. Henry had a job waiting and so, we drove all day to our destination of Walgett, a tiny town in outback New South Wales, hundreds of miles from anywhere. My life was restricted, my days were lonely, and I looked to the sky, asking, 'Why me, God?'

As we drove up the dirt road, all you could see were miles and miles of cotton plants and dirt—there was red-brown dirt as far as the eye could see. The landscape was dotted with tall ghost gums. Every now and then, a white cockatoo would flash its wings and rise up from the saltbush, soaring high into the bright blue sky. We were headed for an old cattle station. The property owner lived there amongst the old houses of the original settlers, which were built right on the edge of the Barwon River. My husband was to be the dozer driver; it was his job to clear more land for cattle or for cotton, whichever the property owner wanted to grow. All I knew about the place we were going to was that the house had not been lived in for years, and a flood had passed through it since it was last occupied.

I stared out the car window. The hot air was blowing in my face and my hair was pulled back to try to escape the smothering feeling of the dry heat. My thoughts turned to our previous home, the tiny caravan from the sapphire mine. I had no idea what had happened to it. All I knew was that it was gone, along with photos and my childhood things—all the treasures I had kept from earlier days. It seems funny when I think back to those days. I was too scared to even ask what my husband had done with our home and possessions. Everything we owned was gone. But things never did mean much to me. We had no furniture and only the barest of possessions: saucepans, plates, knives and forks, sheets, towels, blankets, and clothes. The air was so hot that the dirt just stuck to our skin as it floated in the open windows of the car. The children were tired, hot, and sick of each other's company, so the old house was a welcome sight on the horizon. It was approaching dusk as the old Ford Fairlane pulled into the driveway of the farmhouse.

It was a typical old-style Queenslander house. A large verandah encircled the main house, but someone had closed it in with mesh to stop the mosquitoes. The front door was open, obviously to air the place out; or on second thoughts, maybe it was always open. Who knows? No one had lived there for a very long time. Tonight all we could hope for was a makeshift bed and some tinned food to eat. 'No frills tonight kids,' I called out. Tomorrow we would look at what we could do to make this place home for however long it was going to be. The children didn't care. They were just so excited about being out of the car. They didn't care about beds or food. They screeched and ran and explored every inch of that old house, running from room to room. The sound of their feet echoed on the hard wooden floors.

'Hey, Mum, there's a creek at the back door,' one of them yelled. And sure enough, from the top of the back stairs, all you could see was the deep Barwon River flowing silently at the bottom of steep river banks.

The house was still caked in mud which seemed to have clung to every surface and was visible halfway up the walls. I looked with amazement and wondered how on earth I was going to make this place a home. The kitchen table was large and I would have guessed it was probably about a hundred years old. The walls were green, a dirty olive green. There was one kitchen window looking to the south, just above the ceramic sink with its one simple brass turn-on tap. The house, as I could see it, had one saving grace—a huge wood-burning stove with a hot water tank attached. So at least, there would be hot water and a bath every night. Thank God for small mercies! There were a couple of old metal beds with very old mattresses, and one or two cupboards with drawers. We had electricity, which ran from a generator at the main house, but no extras like lamps or kitchen things. The phone was a hand-ringer type. It was … you know, a shared party line. You had to turn the handle to get an operator on the line to connect you to whoever you wanted to speak with. The phone didn't work, although it had once, and probably would again. For now, just silence was all there was at the other end of the line.

We unpacked our few possessions. What a raggedy bunch of lost souls we must have looked. I managed to get some baked beans on bread together for tea, and everyone ate as if it was the most amazing supper of their lives. We were all hungry and very tired. My husband went off to see his new employer to report in, and left me to organize the house for the night. So I pulled together a couple of the old beds on the verandah, threw a blanket over the dirty old mattresses and then added a clean sheet and pillows. 'Everyone has to sleep in one bed tonight kids, and no arguments,' I said authoritatively. The three of them threw themselves onto the bed, pushing and shoving for the best space. There were giggles and groans, and more giggles as they wriggled themselves into position. 'Mum, she's pulling all the blankets, Mum!'

My response was, 'Enough! It's been a long day, everyone needs some sleep.' Tomorrow would be a new day and a new beginning, and there would be lots of work to do to get this place clean and livable, that was for sure.' That night, we slept so soundly, as though the world were in its perfect place. The noises of the night crept in, and the darkness filled every inch of the landscape. You could not see a sign of life. It was so quiet, and so dark, and so peaceful. I could see the stars shining like diamonds. As I looked out, I found myself thinking, I wonder what's at the end of the sky? Surely something must exist beyond the end!

The next day, we surveyed the house and surroundings. The

whole scene was one of neglect and abandonment. I suppose it was appropriate really, given that the house hadn't been occupied in twenty years. We decided the only way to clean it properly was to use the fire truck and pressure hoses. The kids were exploring, so Henry and I removed anything that could get water damaged and turned on the fire pump. Brooms, water, and good old-fashioned hard work were the measure of the day. We started with the kitchen and then just let it flow. Henry had to go and fill the tanker several times before the day was over. We simply blasted the river mud right out of the house inch by inch.

Finally, most of the mud was gone. Everything was wet but, in this 100 degree heat, it wouldn't take long to dry out. The house smelt like the creek mud–a pungent smell like nothing on earth, and one that seemed to get right into your skin and clothes. It didn't take long before the house was dry, and the beds were pulled into rooms. Then we began searching around the property to see what we could find and reclaim to use as furniture. In the afternoon, the boss turned up in his truck to deliver an old refrigerator, which seemed to work fine, although it surely had seen better days. And so, life began on the station, just as though there had never been a pause in Henry's and my relationship. I lived a simple life, trying to make the old and broken home beautiful. Nature had its gifts—the birds, the creek, and the magnificent night sky.

In spite of all the hardship, there were many happy times. I taught my children at home. We were all together, and although we didn't have much, life was somehow working out a little better. The distractions had been removed, there was a weekly pay cheque, and no one was going hungry. Once in a while I grabbed the chance to relax and paint my pictures, or do some sewing amongst the day-today chores of being a wife and mother. It must have been about a year after that when, late one evening, we had a phone call from our old friends Lee and Rose. They were working on a property down in the Blue Mountains near Oberon. Lee was calling to tell Henry about a good job that was on offer. We were all good friends and the offer was just too good to turn down. It would be good. I would have my best friend back to talk to, and our kids were also such good mates. The move was definitely a step forward. So once again, we packed our bags. This time, we bought a trailer so we could at least take a little more with us, and off we went again.

I hoped and prayed that this move would be one for the better. We would be closer to friends, and the kids could go to a real school again. It was a seven mile rough dirt track down the mountain to the valley where the farmhouses were situated. The property was huge: there were sheep, cows, horses, snakes, and pine trees as far as the eye could see. The house was sort of cozy, not very big, and the laundry and toilet were downstairs in another building; but it had a sort of welcoming vibe. It wasn't long before the kids were all going to school and Henry had settled into his new job. He was working miles away up on the mountains, clearing land to make it ready for planting pine forests. My friend Rose lived next door so we had many cups of tea together. We used to bake the most amazing things to share—custard slices, and sponge cakes. You name it; we cooked it and ate it! Life was simple, living down in the valley below the mountain ridges. But we shared lots of laughter with good company and that somehow made life seem quite normal once more. The normal was not going to last long however. Looking back, I was hardly prepared for the course of events which were about to begin shoving me screaming and kicking towards my destiny.

We hadn't been living in the house long when strange things

began to happen. I would put pictures up on the wall, and they would fly off. I don't mean they fell down, like if a hook fell out. It was as if someone had thrown them across the room. I would put things down, only to go back and find them moved or put away in a cupboard. At first, I just thought I was losing the plot; you know, getting confused or forgetful. That was, until the night I woke with someone sitting next to me on my double bed, and it wasn't Henry! It seemed our house had a permanent resident, a lovely old lady, who seemed to think the house was still her home. The night she woke me was preceded by a normal day, with the kids going to school and me digging and creating the new vegetable garden. Of course, there were the normal things like making beds and cleaning the house, but nothing out of the ordinary occurred. It was coming on to winter, with the prospect of seeing our first snow and everyone was happy.

I had headed off to bed about 8 pm and quickly fallen asleep. The long days and hard work, combined with the fresh mountain air, made it easy to sleep. I'm not sure how long I had been asleep (I had been worried about Henry. He was off drinking with his mates and playing cards again.) when I remember feeling the weight of someone sitting down next to me. Then there was the feeling of someone, so very gently, kissing my forehead. I woke with a start, bleary-eyed, to see the face of an elderly woman looking at me, smiling. She just nodded, smiled, got up, and walked away. I guess she approved of me after all, and was just letting me know in her own way that she was there. After that, just every now and then, I would see her out of the corner of my eye. She seemed very happy to have a family sharing her space. The sensitive spiritual side of me was starting to stir once again, and again I began questioning why life was always so hard, and how I could make it better. I still seemed to suffer from the bizarre, inexplicable nervous disposition which resulted in constant nausea, headaches, and body pain. I was sure tired of always feeling sick. I had this hole in my gut. I don't mean physically, but it was like an energy hole, a feeling of something being missing. I had no idea how to find what it was I needed to fill that hole with.

There was a silent Cold War raging inside of me. It was a fight between the person I had become in order to survive, and the person I really was. Something was not right in my life, and I could no longer ignore the questions running through my mind. I had died that day on the operating table. I had gone to heaven and been told I had to come back and finish what I had come into this life to do. I had no idea what that was, how to make life better, or even how to be happy any more. I had tried for years to ignore the whole thing. I had ignored my flashes of insight and ignored the fact that I lived only for everyone else. I was a mother first, and a wife second. By the end of the day, I was just so tired, and I didn't have any energy left to give anyone, not even myself. Everything was about being who 'they' wanted me to be.

I had no one in my life I could talk to about the deep things—the questions I had about life and death, and the spiritual things that haunted me. They were just too much for most people, even my friend Rose. I made a few new friends in the local town. Julie and Keith lived in the little town up the hill; they had a little boy and two daughters. Tragedy struck one day when the little boy was playing with his dog near the dam at the side of their house. Somehow, he slipped in and drowned; it was awful. My heart went out to Julie and Keith; they worshiped that little boy. The empathy I felt for them was so strong, it would open a doorway that I would never be able to close. My opening up to things beyond the physical in this instance, all started when I walked into their house for the gathering after the funeral. As I walked into the room, the little boy's picture was facing me on the stand. In a flash, the picture began to transform before my eyes and, as clear as day, on his forehead shone a large silver cross. I was shocked! Everyone noticed the look on my face. I watched as his picture continued to change. Now he was there in the photo, smiling and laughing, just as though he were alive. 'Julie,' I gasped, 'can you see that?' I pointed at the photograph, and everyone stopped. They could see it too. The photo had somehow changed and permanently taken on the mark of a crucifix on the little boy's forehead. This was surely a sign—sign that he was in the care of the Lord in heaven.

I had never seen anything like that before; it was confusing to say the least. I didn't know what was happening to me. Was I going mad? I had no one in the physical world to guide me and show me how to find the answers. I needed to work out for myself, why I was born and what my life was all about. I needed to put my life in order somehow. I prayed for guidance and came to the conclusion I needed time to think so I could come up with some answers. That was where it had to begin, a brief window of time each day for me to be in my own head space, just a few minutes for me. So, I decided that I would wait until the house was quiet, the children were at school, and Henry was at work. I thought the important thing was to get my thoughts in order, so I began to write, just scribbles of thoughts in a notebook. My mind raced … what if someone found my notes and read them? This thought scared me to death. So my first conscious battle in my search for answers was about overcoming irrational fears that could stop me from writing my thoughts in a journal—it was that simple. Thank God, I did find the courage to keep writing. For that simple act of beginning to journal my dreams and thoughts, was to be the first key to searching for, and finding the knowledge which would enable me to heal and restore my life.

T.B. HUMAN

Winters were extremely cold down in the valley; snow covered the peaks, and the weather was not conducive to going outdoors. Rain often followed the snow and when it rained, the roads became impassable to ordinary cars. Only the four-wheel drive trucks held any chance of getting through to the town on the ridge above. I had many hours to myself just to do what I did best; that was, to contemplate the universe and the question of why I was born into this life. I had no idea what my mission was, but I sure wasn't going to give up on finding out. I had to finish what I started. But what had I started? That was the burning question of my life.

Each afternoon, I would find that hour, that space in which I could relax and ponder the universe. I always began simply by sitting quietly and closing my eyes. I would allow whatever thoughts wanted to come into my head, to just appear. Then I would begin to write. I didn't care whether it made sense or not. The important thing was that I was beginning to express my deepest thoughts, and no one else e v e r had to know.

Spiritual practices were something no one ever spoke about; that was something one did in private and kept totally to oneself. I had been catching glimpses of spirit beings for most of my life. I found it strangely odd that the only people who had mentioned anything about spirit to me were generally people who were dying. When I worked as a nurse back in the early days of my marriage, that particular fact was one thing that struck me as a common theme. I noticed how my patients who were not far from death, always mentioned seeing people in spirit waiting for them, as though to assist them through the transition. On the other hand, I seemed to see people who wanted to get messages to those left behind, or people who had died suddenly, and had somehow got stuck between worlds. These things were part of my everyday reality.

Also, in the early days of my spiritual practices, I found it very easy to do astral travel[5]. When my energy was being adjusted and my senses were developing, I would get so tired; all I wanted to do was sleep, which I did, and the hours would just slip away. But when I slept, there were times when I felt as though I could hardly stay in my body. So I would leave it behind and just float away into other realms. There, I would experience other realities and other ways of thinking. I often felt as though I was traveling through time to retrieve precious insights from past lives. It was as though I had opened Pandora's Box and every possible type of experience had been released, each revealing a far more in-depth and complicated view of the world in which we all resided. I wanted to know how all my experiences fitted together. And not only that, but also, what on earth I was meant to do with all this information.

I knew I had to become more self-aware, and to watch my thoughts and see where they led me. But sometimes there would be so many thoughts that my head felt as if it was turning inside out; the thoughts would all jumble together in a confused state of disarray. At times, I honestly began to wonder about my sanity. Did everyone think like this? If they did, no wonder the world was in such a mess. My mind seemed intent on thinking of all sorts of crazy scenarios, most of which never actually happened. My thoughts were constantly about tomorrow or yesterday and 'What if ... ?' or 'If only ... '.

---

[5] Wikipedia defines astral body is a subtle body posited by many religious philosophers. **Astral journey (or *astral trip*)** is the same as having an *out-of-body experience*. Astral projection and the astral plane are a controversial interpretation of out-of-body experiences. Astral catalepsy is a type of catalepsy and sort of sleep paralysis which, under some circumstances at a semi-awake state, can be experienced in connection with an astral journey.

My mind was going quite crazy, not only about 'What will people think?' but also about 'How am I doing?' The questions just kept crashing in. But I stuck with it, and it wasn't long before the first real clues to the direction I needed to follow began to emerge; I realized I was at the mercy of an overactive mind. It was a bit like being in the middle of the city markets at eight o'clock on a Sunday morning, with everyone going in different directions all at once. It was as though my thoughts ran me, rather than me being able to focus my thoughts. So with my first realization in hand (i.e. that I needed to be able to control and focus my thoughts), I turned my mind to finding the next clue.

It was important for me to find a way to express what I was feeling inside. I knew I wanted my life to change as it was just too awful for it to stay the way it was. My determination pushed me onwards. There was a longing to understand. Life was so lonely, as the only companionship I had was that of my children and my good friend Rose. I think the universe works in a crazy way. It seems to use pain and unhappiness to motivate us. But I really think, if life were easy, would anyone question anything? The more I gave of myself to my family, the more they expected of me and wanted from me. I lived for everyone else and tried to keep everyone else happy. Life just continued to be irrationally miserable and I felt like I was losing all sense of myself. I was sinking deeper and deeper into loneliness. My children were by now growing up and finding their own feet, and the family seemed to be no longer the most important thing in the world to them. I was beginning to feel the oncoming, inevitable empty nest looming ahead of me.

My logic may have been flawed, but this is how I began to find my way. I considered, that if my body were a compass, happiness meant I was aligned to my own true north. Then, the way I was feeling about life, meant that somehow I must be currently facing the wrong way. If I could work out what was true for me, and then live aligned to that sense of rightness, my life would be happier. So, what made up that sense of rightness? I thought about it for days and finally came to the realization I needed so desperately. The Knights creed states: courage, honesty, integrity, thoughtfulness and forgiveness—kindness, above all; and to protect those who are old, frail or weak.

If my life was not happy, I thought … well, I must have made choices in the past which did not align to the creed; hence, I was not standing in my truth of spirit at the time. Surely if I could be one hundred percent honest with myself, and follow only the direction that felt absolutely true and right in my heart, then I must attract people with that same honesty into my life. Life had to get better, didn't it!

So that is where my spiritual journey really started. Step one, was beginning to write a journal which helped me to realize how bizarre my life had become. And step two, was beginning to find my truth. What I needed to know was where I had gone wrong. Where had I not had the courage to stand by what my conscience told me was right?

To answer this question, there was only one place I could look in my experience, and that was within. I reviewed my situation and affirmed that I was lost, lonely, sad, and incredibly unhappy. To the world, there was no reason for being this way. After all, it appeared I was married to a good man and I had three healthy, happy children. And yet, I felt like I was dying inside. It was as if there was numbness or an emptiness that nothing could fill. I felt like there was someone else I would rather be. The person I was right now, in the life I was living, just wasn't working for me, no matter how hard I tried to make it perfect.

There was only one answer for it. I always knew I had a destiny; I always thought there was a reason for being alive. All I had to do was to find out what I was born to do. At that time in my life, my health was very erratic. I was always feeling sick, and no doctor could identify what was wrong with me. I lost track of how many doctor's visits there had been. Every week I had been; some weeks involved more than one visit to the surgery. I felt utterly ridiculous, but I was still no closer to working out why I was so unwell and so tired; there had to be something wrong! It was the middle of the afternoon, and I was feeling more than a little uneasy about facing the doctor once more. When I did find the courage to go, it was obvious he thought I was just another neurotic woman. He looked at me blankly and said, 'I can't find anything wrong with you. Take this medication to help you relax, and see how you go. If this doesn't work, we'll do some more tests. So make sure you come back to see me next week.' Yes, take another darned pill, and hopefully it will all just go away; but I knew it wouldn't!

I sat in the waiting room of the doctor's surgery on that cold winter's day, wondering why any of us were born at all. Is there any purpose to the inner struggle, the emotions? What if somewhere, I had taken the wrong turn? What if I had missed my destiny? What if I am not the person I am supposed to be? Why do I feel so unwell all the time? Maybe, if life had been different, could I have been someone else? What if I am really meant to do something, or be someone else, but I've never learnt how to be that person? What if I have a purpose? What if I am not in the right place at the right time? What do I want to do with my life? These were the thoughts that flooded my mind that day.

There is something about winter that brings us to a point of reflection. In winter, all growth stops, and the garden seems to wait for the first kiss of spring warmth to caress the ground, in order for life to once again spring forth. As strange as it sounds, I felt as though I was in a winter, just like the plants in the garden. It was me who waited quietly in the winter snow, praying that soon the sun would shine and life would blossom in a way it had never blossomed before. The Central Tablelands had endured a long harsh winter that year, and just like the landscape, the quiet, cold stagnation of my life seemed to go on and on, with no sign of ending. How could I change things? What would I do, if I could do anything? Who would I want to be? There were so many questions and no answers. All I felt was a gaping great hole in my gut where my soul should have been.

At first, I tried to solve my dilemma logically. I rationalized that if I could find my purpose, a job or a career that fulfilled me, then I would have to be happier. Yes, having a purpose would help me escape the worries and thoughts going 'round and 'round in my busy head. Maybe, if I could find the answers to all these questions, the confusion would disappear. Maybe all the problems of life would be easier to handle and my troubles would be far behind me. When I thought about it, I didn't really know what I wanted to leave behind. Some days I wanted to escape the hurt and loneliness in my marriage. Sometimes, it was the anger Henry inflicted on the children and me. His anger triggered my anger, which in turn left me feeling trapped and helpless.

Why had my life turned out to be so unhappy? Why had this happened to me God? I had always tried to be a good person, and I never wanted to hurt anyone. There just seemed to be so much injustice about everything that existed in my life. Surely I was born to be loved, to be nurtured, and to have someone think of me as their special someone. I just wanted to be like any other young woman, not having responsibility for others and the never-ending expectations and demands of being a mother and a wife. Life was suffocating me so much that I felt as though I was wrapped with invisible strings that held me prisoner in an invisible jail and there was no escape.

If only I could fly far away from it all and just feel like I was alive, rather than an extension of everyone else. Our marriage was mostly miserable. It hadn't been going well for some time. We rarely laughed or joked; or for that matter, even talked about anything meaningful. There were always the pressures of money and work, and the problem that Henry's mates came first, and so did his drinking. I couldn't really remember when it had been any other way. There never seemed to be enough money to pay the bills, and buying a house while raising three children was quite impossible. My husband was drinking more, spending more, and worrying less. We had reached a precarious point where our relationship was miserable for both of us. But there were the children, and try as I may to leave; every time, he would just drag me back. Threats, a loaded Magnum 22 Hornet, and empty promises—I could not put my children through it again. I had to stay and make it work, for their sake.

I tried so hard to be a perfect wife, hoping my husband would notice and want to spend time with me, but he didn't. Henry seemed intent on avoiding me whenever he could. He didn't understand what was wrong with our relationship. His way of dealing with it was to go hunting or fishing. So he would withdraw and spend as much time as he could being far away from the children and me. I was lost and lonely, and life felt so empty. Women deal with their emotions; they seek comfort and love when unhappy. Men, on the other hand, want to fix things; and if they don't know how to fix things, they feel inadequate. What we actually had was a no-win situation. We loved each other, but had no idea of 'how' to love each other. At that time in my life, the only thing that kept me going was my love for my children; they were everything to me. And, I kept myself constantly busy.

We lived miles from town, but I managed to get a job doing manual labor on the farm. That kept me so tired that I didn't feel or think. Without realizing it, I was becoming addicted to being busy, a habit that would stay with me the rest of my life. Keeping myself busy filled the great big void of emptiness inside me. I didn't work to live; I lived to work. Every waking moment had to be productive. My house had to be clean and my children taken care of. As a result, my health began to deteriorate even more: there were colds, sore throats, stomach pains, back pains, and headaches. My whole body, mind, and spirit felt out of sorts. I felt exhausted and so unwell all the time. There was one mysterious complaint after the other. And secretly, there was lack of love and affection, and constant conflict.

Looking back, I was actually worrying myself to death inch by inch. I worried that maybe I really had some rare disease that the doctor kept overlooking. Many years before, I had contracted a rare virus called brucellosis from drinking unprocessed cow's milk. And once I had cat scratch fever from a wild cat on the farm. But secretly, I worried I had some deadly parasite! Imagination is a powerful thing when you're afraid.

What I noticed was, my mind seemed to keep on playing this stupid no-win game. No matter how much I tried to escape my worries, my thoughts just kept on slipping back into my 'What-if?' mindset. At times, I wanted to scream, 'Shut up!' to the crazy thoughts going 'round and 'round in my head. Every time I was confronted by a challenge, my head went crazy. What if this happens? What if that happens? And of course, you know what people will say. I was being driven absolutely nuts with all of my own insecurities and there was absolutely no escape.

I watched my friends being happy with loving husbands. I watched the smiles, the laughter, and the gentle touches. And I cried, there was none of that for me. All our marriage was about was just plain old fashioned sex. That was all he ever wanted from me. Plain and simple, take it or leave it. Close your eyes and think of England! Why didn't he love me? Why didn't he want me? Why didn't he nurture me? My thoughts raced, and finding the solution to the problem seemed impossible.

I was a beautiful woman and yet I felt so ugly and awkward. My hair was long, down past my waist, and I had a fine figure 37-24-34. I only weighed eight stone, but I was as strong as any man and could work equally as hard. And that was not all; I was skilled in the kitchen and could easily cook the most delicious food. I loved my home and kept it neat and clean as a show home. We didn't have much of anything, no flashy furniture or car, but I always made things look nice. Once I even made some furniture; I found an old Reader's Digest 'How to…' instruction book and set to building two verandah lounge chairs. I went and bought the wood and canvas, and they were exactly like the pictures when I finished.

But it didn't seem to matter how much I did, it was never enough. Never, ever, did I manage to find approval in his eyes! He just lived in his own world of work and fishing and drinking— always. I did wonder sometimes how it felt to be him. Maybe he just didn't need tenderness and love. I didn't know any more. So many thoughts …

In the midst of that afternoon back in the doctor's waiting room, I had the courage to take the first really honest look at my life. All the confusion and outdated beliefs had to go. I had to find out how to be myself and let go of this emotional chaos. I needed to find peace within myself. Who am I? I am my father's and mother's daughter. I am Henry's wife. I am my children's mother. But who am I really?

With this honesty, came the extremely unnerving realization that I didn't know very much about who I really was—inside. The more I questioned, the more uncomfortable I felt, like a pressure cooker about to explode. Or, as though there was something just too big, too incomprehensible, too indefinable that my head was trying to grasp. I began to sob uncontrollably. In truth, I just didn't know where to start to fix things. I didn't know any other way to live except to take care of everyone else, and that put my needs last on the list. My days were each the same as the day before. I felt as though I had become caught up in Groundhog Day. Every moment was spent taking care of what everyone else needed; always trying to keep things perfect, clean and tidy, healthy and nice. Taking care of my family's needs had taken over my life and sadly, it was all that I knew how to do: washing, ironing, cooking, cleaning, and paying the bills; bathing and feeding the children, tending to the animals, mowing the lawn, and doing the gardening to grow the vegetables. This existence surely wasn't how I thought life would be. I had imagined travel and a career … not that I regretted my children; I could not imagine life without them. I think it was more the isolation, the loneliness, and the fact I just felt I had no personal fulfillment.

I felt so unraveled and I struggled to regain my composure. I had this feeling like something deep in my gut nagged at me. It was like a deep memory calling me to wake up, as though I had something I should remember; but I couldn't, for the life of me, recall what it was.

I had wandered over to the magazine rack in the corner and absentmindedly picked up a rather tatty looking 'New Idea' Magazine. My eyes tried to focus, but my mind seemed to be intent on being elsewhere; it was a strange sensation, like being there but not being there. The eternal question occupied my mind: What am I searching for and what on earth is wrong with me? It wasn't comfortable being here in this life; or for that matter, being once again in the doctor's office. The room was filled with all manner of people—some old, some young, some spluttering and coughing, and others looking just as miserable as I felt. After I picked up the magazine from the pile, I quietly slipped back into my chair without really looking at anyone; I was embarrassed at feeling so fragile. As I flicked through the magazine, my eyes skimmed over the glossy pictures and the well-worn pages without really absorbing anything. I skipped a few pages, and just as I was about to throw the magazine onto the table, I noticed, of all things, a large partly finished crossword puzzle just a few pages from the back of the magazine.

There must have been at least a dozen different pens used to fill in these squares. Others before me had added their precious insights in an attempt to complete this particular puzzle. My eyes caught sight of one row of empty, little white boxes on the page. There was just one line left to complete the challenge, but no one before me had managed to do it. I looked at the space number and then back up to the reference questions for a clue to the missing word.

42 Down: In what movie was the answer given to the meaning

of life? I searched my mind for the right answer, but it eluded me. How peculiar, the question was exactly what I had been thinking about when I picked up the magazine. In the next moment, a sharp voice broke my train of thought, 'Lesley, the doctor will see you now.'

I bolted from my seat like a startled cat and threw the magazine back onto the coffee table. A nervous smile flashed as I nodded toward the receptionist and headed through the doctor's open door. Instantaneously, I had been brought back to the reality of the moment, and my attention became consumed with just trying to cope, by not dissolving into puddles of tears once again.

And so, life continued with normal routines until … my older sister came to visit me. It was one of those rare occasions when she was at loose ends in between relationships, and I guess she just needed some family time with her little sister. I could talk to my sister. She was somewhat like me, in that she had also experienced things beyond what people called normal; in fact, she was quite intuitive. Like me, Patricia had a profoundly creative side; she worked as a potter and an artist. She was also a lover of nature and all things natural—always looking for ways to improve her health and well-being. While we did share many things in common, we were not close, not the way I thought sisters should be. The age gap between us was fourteen years, and when we moved to Australia, she was at the age of getting on with life and left home. I never had her around after the age of four, but she used to spoil me every chance she got by bringing me gifts and trying to be the sister I always wanted her to be.

One afternoon, we were sitting in the sun on the verandah, just enjoying the warmth and peace, when I decided I should share what had been going on in my life. So I plucked up the courage and told her about my strange and bizarre experiences (my near-death experience in 1976 and all the stuff that had gone on since). My sister looked straight at me and said, 'There is a book you should read. It will help you understand. The book is called *Reaching for the Other Side* by Dawn Hill.' My sister, being the helper she was, gifted me the book and I just devoured it. I was so astounded at Dawn Hill's journey and how similar it was to mine that I wrote to her. To my surprise, she wrote back. Dawn suggested I get in touch with a lady named Jenny, who she felt could help me harness my gifts.

So began my true journey. Jenny was, and is to this day, someone I immensely respect; I am so thankful for her presence in my life. Over the next months, I underwent a ten-step personal development program which Jenny had written. Very long letters flowed back and forth between us, and questions were answered deep within my soul. Jen had amazing perception. Her ability to unravel the challenges I faced was astounding, and she told me she had never had a student develop in consciousness so fast. I am sure, sometimes she wondered if I would just fly off into the ether and get lost in a world of psychic confusion and illusion combined. This would have probably been the case if Jenny had not helped me ground my ability and learn the essential basics of safe, practical, personal spiritual development. In the beginning, the tasks were simple—sit quietly for a few minutes every day, allow myself to relax and let go of all my worries and thoughts. The aim of this was so that my mind would become quiet, for the endless chatter in my head went on and on, most of the time—what to do about this, what to do about that, what would someone think of this, and what would someone think about that. It was just a constant jumble of thoughts, all of which were totally a waste of energy. My mind was like a pure-bred race horse running backwards around the racetrack.

We didn't have Internet in those days. We were lucky to have a manual telephone with a shared extension. I learnt to meditate[6], initially to release stress and calm the mind. Later, I learnt how to move beyond the physical world to connect with my higher self, my guides, and my guardians. I learnt to view my life as though I were the watcher of its progress. And in that, I found I could solve issues, heal old hurts, and still hold on to the reality of the world we all have to live within. I learnt how to stay grounded[7].

I have found that many people find it very difficult to stay grounded; their thoughts are so scattered that they sometimes find it hard to complete even simple tasks. Grounding is an easy technique to learn and it is not hard to do when you know how. In those early days, when my skills were growing extremely fast, I learnt how certain foods could help make your body energy work more effectively. Some foods help to ground the energy to the physical, while others (e.g. anything to do with alcohol) tends to do the opposite. Chocolate is a great grounding tool. I can hear you laughing right now, saying, 'No wonder I love chocolate so much. Now I have an excuse to eat it'. Yet, if eaten to excess, it can do the opposite, simply because of the sugar content. For example, children

---

[6] Wikipedia defines **meditation** is a practice in which an individual trains the mind or induces a mode of consciousness, either to realize some benefit or as an end in itself. The term *meditation refers to a broad variety of practices much like the term sports that include techniques designed to promote relaxation, build internal energy or life force (qi, ki, prana, etc.) and develop compassion, love, patience, generosity, and forgiveness.

[7] Grounded means to restrict or keep restricted, keep attached to earth surface, get to the deepest core of thoughts and ideas, and keep in the reality of life and not lose hold on normal life.

who eat lots of sweets are often ungrounded. They rush about making a lot of noise and seem not to be able to sit still for a moment.

Jenny's simple training program set the bar for the basic principles and techniques that I use to this day. She kept my feet on the ground while my head was in the clouds. She was a godsend by spirit—right time, and right place. I felt like a giant sponge, and I just could not gather enough information to answer my never-ending stream of questions. I learned the skill of empathy; it was easy to use my perceptual skills to know exactly what was happening in another person's life and body. I had no idea what to do with this skill, but it made life very interesting, to say the least.

Winter passed and summer arrived; the heat was incredible throughout the long days. The valley where Henry and I were living had been a rich gold and copper mining area during the gold rush days of Australia (in the 1800s). There were rich mineral deposits deep in the earth which made the ironstone and shale prime targets for lighting strikes in the summer season of storms. Every summer's day ended with a violent storm; the lightning just loved the shale rock, sparking frequent fires upon it. The next year would fly past quickly. My new-found passion was leading me to read books and search out magazines by the dozen. Slowly, I began to regain control over my reactions to other people's behavior and unkind words. I became more and more aware of how my responses to emotional triggers were in fact destroying my peace. My curiosity about spiritual techniques grew. I didn't want to be a psychic; that thought scared the heck out of me. But I did want to learn more about my intuition and how I could become absolutely 100 per cent connected to the power it could potentially bring.

Henry worked hard as always, and played hard too, making many friends in the local town area. Hunting and fishing were a way of life when the men were not working. Bush men love nothing better than to drink hard, play hard, fish hard, and whatever. Nothing was done half-heartedly; everything was all or nothing. As for the children, they learnt about farming, horses, fishing, and growing vegetables. They learnt to survive the dangers of the bush: the snakes, the spiders, and the machinery. One thing I can say is, that at least they had a really good practical upbringing. They all knew how to ride a horse, milk a cow, grow food, and catch fish. They all learnt how to shoot, how to drive, and what to do when there was an emergency. Country life is very different from city life. Everyone knows everyone, and everyone looks out for everyone else. I have missed that sense of community over the years when I have lived in suburbia. In the city I felt as though I had no connection to others. There was no sense of community and everyone seemed so closed off to everything and everybody else. The heart is what connects and heals life. That is something I have learnt over my lifetime. Without the heart, there is no connection to others, and no healing. Our wellness is generated from the nurturing which ultimately comes from our tribe. Even if that tribe is scattered to the four winds, with the modern technology we have today, we can still generate that connection to each other. That love and mutual contact are the keys for all life; without these, the world will fail to thrive and mankind will ultimately perish.

In 1986 opportunity knocked once more. Our friends had left sometime earlier to move back to a small coastal community near Coffs Harbour. Late one evening, a phone call came from them, telling us about this lovely town where there was plenty of work and lots of sea and sand. Without much thought, once again we uprooted our tiny family and moved, this time to a beautiful seaside town on the Mid-North Coast of New South Wales. Before too long, Henry found work as a plant operator, driving a backhoe. The children were quickly growing up and finding their own way. By this time, I had begun holding a spiritual development circle each Sunday night, at which I shared my experiences with my first-time students. Through running this circle, I discovered that there were more people just like me out there in the world. The more I shared, the more I grew in consciousness, and my self-awareness kept on growing. It was at this time that I began investigating the topic of reincarnation; I found the whole theory absolutely fascinating.

My guardians were watching closely, and little by little I began getting little glimpses of knowing what my next step in life and personal growth would be. My writing skills were so limited and it concerned me that this might be a block to my progress. The learning disability from childhood still had me embarrassed and ashamed—I had so much trouble with the comprehension and application of the written word. As is often the case though, where one skill is weak, another compensates by becoming stronger, and I found that my innate communication with God began to develop. Despite its difficulties, writing was the only way available to me to record my thoughts. A scruffy, old pink notebook left over from my son's school days became my very first journal (I still have it somewhere here in the boxes of treasures.).

Each day, I would ask a question about life. And each day I would sit, get my own thoughts out of the way, and just write whatever came into my mind in answer. It took a great deal of practice, but I knew no one was ever going to read it. So it didn't matter what I wrote really, or how badly the words were spelt or formed. The important thing was that I began to listen in to the stillness of the universe, looking for understanding. At first, it was a lot of gobbledygook. It really didn't make much sense and my mind always kept butting in to the conversation. It was only after months of commitment that I began to notice—when I put myself into a light meditative space of no thoughts, the words would just flow. They were beautiful words of reassurance and wisdom, beautiful words from a far greater being than myself.

In allowing myself to be open to this other-worldly communication, my rigid personality was beginning to take a back seat. The answers I received back to my soul-searching questions were always simple and profound. It was as though I was being taught, without being told outright what to do. The teaching was conducted in such a way that it required me to explore every belief and aspect I had previously thought to be true. The burning urge to write about these experiences began to pull me as strongly as a compass needle points to true north. I had no idea how I would master the calling. You see, I had failed English at school. I could read, but with great difficulty. And my grammar ... well now, that was really something else! Australian slang is part of everyday life and no one bothers with punctuation or the proper choice of verbs or adjectives. I had a calling, and thank God I was stubborn enough to endure the pain of learning which was to follow! That stubbornness would enable me to find my calling and to become what it beckoned me to be, and to do.

It was as though my life was being guided, not only by my spirit guardians, but also by something much more powerful in the form of my dreams. They haunted me; night after night there was no reprieve. All those dreams, those haunting memories kept flooding in, and it was as though past lives were calling to me to remember. I would wake, longing for a love lost in another world, another era. I felt as though another Lesley existed somewhere out there in space and time. I watched her in my dreams; I knew her, and it was as though something unfinished haunted her soul, and somehow cut through time and space to enter my world. A young man called David, who had a fierce personality, also haunted my dreams. Stubborn, intelligent, creative—his skills, as well as the words he spoke, were a complete opposite to the life I lived. I began to question the limits of life, and in fact, what if we all have lived before? There was only one course of action to take. I would write down everything I could remember from my dream states of the night before, in the hope that I could discover some consistent or recurring themes.

In no time at all, I had identified several of my key past lives. So many dreams, sometimes of lives coming to a violent end; the intensity of their power would shock and shatter my physical body for days on end. One such memory was of a French queen being led to execution. I could see, feel and smell everything in that dream. I quivered as my head was placed in the guillotine, and I heard the swoosh of the blade as it fell. The astounding thing was that a person would still have consciousness when the head was severed from the body; this was something I had never consciously considered. As my head rolled into the cane basket, I could still think, I could still see, and I could hear the jeers of the crowd. But that was not all; I had a knowing that my head had been severed from my body and my life was no more! That dream haunted me for days, and although I rationalized it as being an overactive imagination, I wondered at the information it revealed.

Before long, it became apparent that I could go one step further than analyzing my dreams. It was never enough for me to have vague theories; I wanted proof that past life was real. To do this, I would have to be able to identify someone I had been in a past life but had no knowledge of. I would have to seek out exact tangible and provable information that I could not know any other way. I wanted names—of real people who had been recorded in documentation or had been publicly recognized historical figures.

One afternoon, I was having my usual meditation time. Normally, I would sit in the specified seated position to meditate, but today I had chosen to lie on my bed where my body could relax a little more. I seemed to drift off very quickly to another place and another time. I have no idea how I tapped into it but to this day, I can remember that experience with such clarity, and the whole scene felt so familiar. I could hear the rhythmic clip-clop of horse's hooves on a cobbled street, the chatter of voices, and the squawks of seagulls. What I was sensing was so real, it was as though I was there. I don't know if I was prepared for what was about to be revealed, but this is exactly how it happened: I knew I was a man in a suit, with a vest and pocket watch. There was a hat perched on my head; a trilby, I think they were called. I seemed preoccupied with events of the day. It was funny, but I remember looking at my heavy brown leather shoes and my pinstripe trousers and thinking, 'My Lord, I am a man!' I was certain, without knowing how or why, that I was very outspoken. I knew I worked for a newspaper, and I had the sense of being a writer (In my present lifetime, being a writer was so far removed from reality that it was almost hilarious. Remember, I could barely read and write, let alone be a journalist of some sort.). Although I had no wife or children of my own, I had a sister who I loved very much. I remember approaching a building and turning to walk inside when a vice of a man, shouted ... I glanced sideways, seeing a man pointing a gun. There was a puff of smoke and the bullet slapped me squarely in the chest, BANG!

I felt a punch as the bullet penetrated my body. Then, with a thud, I fell to the ground. A warm, sticky rush of blood was trickling down my chest. I was in shock. Damn! I had been shot! Panic stricken, my hand gingerly reached up towards where the bullet had struck; I could feel the blood oozing down the left side of my chest. I knew I was about to die. And, at that exact moment of recognition, my physical body, in this lifetime, snapped awake. The experience had been so real; I absolutely thought I had been shot while lying on my bed. Reaching my right hand up to my chest, I was astonished to find there was no blood. I gasped for breath. It is funny to think about that now, but I remember so clearly, touching my chest with my fingers and tentatively looking to see if there was actually blood. Relieved that there was none, I felt confused and shocked at the vividness of the experience. One thing was for certain though—it would leave me with no doubt that, yes, we have lived before; and yes, we could very well access those other lives and reap from them, skills that we can use to complement our present lives.

Who was that? What on earth was that all about? I clearly heard from outside my body the name, David Graham Phillips. Who on earth was David Graham Phillips? I had no idea. The name just echoed in my head over and over, and over again. I was a country girl living in Australia who had failed English at school and hated history. We only watched local television. I had never been overseas except for being born in London, and I had no knowledge of America or American history. So who was this man, the man whose body I had occupied at the time of his death?

As I said before, there was no Internet in those days. Communications and research were limited to good old-fashioned books. So a few days later, off to the local library I trotted, determined to try to find some proof that this person had lived. But, to be honest, I doubted if I would ever find anything. Where to start? Ok, the obvious place would have to be the encyclopedia. If this man were anyone of importance, he would surely be listed there. And sure enough, to my absolute astonishment, he was. The following is, in brief, what I finally found in the old, red encyclopedia:

David Graham Phillips 31 October 1867 – 24 January 1911. Born in Madison, Indiana, he was a newspaper reporter in Cincinnati, Ohio before moving to New York. He graduated from high school and went on to attend Princeton University in 1887. Phillips wrote a novel *The Great God Success that* was published in 1901. The royalty income enabled him to work as a freelance journalist while continuing to write fiction. Phillips' novels often commented on social issues of the day and frequently chronicled events based on his real-life journalistic experiences. He was considered a progressive and a muckraker. While writing articles for various prominent magazines, he began to develop a reputation as a competent investigative journalist. David Graham Philips is known for leading one of the most important investigations. He exposed details of corruption of the senate by big business; in particular, by the Standard Oil Company. He was among a few other writers during that time who helped prompt President Theodore Roosevelt to use the term *muckrakers*. Phillips' reputation cost him his life in January 1911, when he was shot outside the Princeton Club at Gramercy Park in New York City. The killer was a Harvard-educated musician named Fitzhugh Coyle Goldsborough. He was a violinist in the Pittsburgh Symphony

Orchestra who came from a prominent Maryland family. Goldsborough believed that Phillips's novel, *The Fashionable Adventures of Joshua Craig*, had cast literary aspersions on his family. After David died, his sister Carolyn organized his final manuscript for posthumous publication using the title, *Susan Lenox: Her Fall and Rise*. In 1931, the book would be made into an MGM motion picture.

Quotes: Fellow, Anthony R. "American Media History: Second Edition" Wadsworth. Boston, MA. 2005.   H.L. Mencken, My Life as Author and Editor, p. 129.

References:

F. T. Cooper, Some American Story-Tellers, (New York, 1911)

J. C. Underwood, Literature and Insurgency, (New York, 1914)

The day I found out about my past life as David Graham Phillips (i.e. that I had been a person who had achieved some things in life, and was even a writer), left me questioning everything I thought was reality. I questioned my place in this world and the fact that in this life I was just an ordinary woman (a mother, and soon to be a grandmother). From that day onwards, my life path was being set. Here I was, a woman with no education, who had a burning inexplicable desire to make a difference. I was a woman who had to find her path and then I was determined to go on to push the barriers as far as it was possible to push them. I had no doubt that I could do it; my DNA had just been hot-wired. But little did I understand the significance of the realization I had discovered and the new direction I was committing myself to. Life was about to become even more bizarre; it was like I was Alice in Wonderland and I had fallen down the rabbit hole. And so, I contemplated life. What was it I was supposed to do? How on earth was I going to find it?

Sitting in the sunroom on the verandah of the old house where we lived, I decided I needed to take some control. Only I could steer my life; I had to decide where it was headed. Up until then, I had, more randomly than consciously, been following the bouncing ball along the corridor which was my life's path. I had been opening every doorway to see what lay beyond and I had been questioning every experience. But still, I had not found happiness. Now, at last, I felt that my life was leading me somewhere; I knew that, but where? I guess I would work that out when I came to it. The afternoon sun streamed through the window, warming the room, but also my body and my bones; it took me into a blissfully relaxed space. The thought came to mind that maybe I should write a mission statement for my life. I reasoned that if I knew clearly what I wanted to achieve, and allowed it to guide my actions; then surely, if I were to die, at least I would have had a darned good shot at doing what I was born to do. Things had changed. On that day, I made up my mind to stop asking, 'What am I supposed to do?' and began announcing to the universe *what I wanted to do*. From then on, I was going to set my own benchmarks. So I reached for my notebook and pen, and began to write the words to explain how I felt at that moment. I began to put a small paragraph together about how I would live my life. These are the words I wrote that day:

'I want to heal my life, and in doing so, help others to have the courage to do the same. I want to help others to be able to help themselves. I want to be free of the confusion and the pain and live my life in love, not fear. I want to find out who I really am. I want to do everything I came into this life to do; I want to be able to leave this life one day with no regrets. I want to know the TRUTH.'

It was this simple statement which said it all. The months that followed were like a landslide of developmental growth. I would barely have time to put my feet on the solid ground of understanding when another insight into life, health, the body's energy system, or healing would unfold. In the weeks that followed, my old friend, my guardian, my watcher—Apari Orad—had returned to my life. Every day, he stood under the very large mango tree at the back of our house. Every day, the silent sentinel was watching, without movement or comment. I thought I was the only one who could see him, but I was wrong. One Sunday night, one of the ladies from our group, Maureen, went up to the kitchen to get some hot water for the coffee. She came back looking rather perplexed as she blurted out, 'Bloody hell! Who is that Aboriginal man standing outside?' Maureen made a face; her eyes looked as if they were going to pop out of her head. 'He's a tall bugger, isn't he? Standing there with all his paint on and feathers tied on his ankles. What does he want?' she kept on asking.

I just smiled, saying, 'Well, I don't really know. He just stands there, watching me. I think he is checking me out for something, but I am not sure what (Generally, spirit will watch to see if you are the person they will ask to complete a task for them.). He appears every day, and that's where he stays, just standing like a statue.' I just shook my head, thinking of the first time I had seen him and wondering why he chose to watch over me. I guess there must be a bigger picture, and after just experiencing the past life of David Graham Phillips, that was part of the bigger picture too. I had no idea where all of this knowledge was headed, or even if it was headed anywhere.

Time rolled swiftly by as days turned into weeks and weeks turned into months. My relationship with Henry seemed to go in cycles; we would get along well for a while, and then the tension would begin to build. We would start fighting and Henry would drink more, and behave worse. At times he acted like the town fool. He even went so far as to set his boss's boots on fire one day while drinking at the hotel; he thought it was funny! We had what was called a 'honeymoon cycle' going on; we would makeup, and then break up, and then do it all again. Was there ever to be an end to it? Meanwhile, I longed for company, for intelligent conversation, and for the affection he had stopped giving me long ago. I wanted to have a good relationship. I wanted love and understanding, someone to join me on my journeys into the unknown and someone who actually liked my company. I was about to learn: you have to be careful what you wish for, because you just might receive it, if you are not careful.

My dreams were big, but they were not complicated and there were days when I thought I had accomplished some of what I had set out to do. At other times, I just felt that life was a mess of confusion and emotions; there was so much emotional pain at that time that I felt like a train wreck. It took time to learn about myself and the complexity of who I was. I knew that the only way my life was going to get better was if I could get things right, inside of me, and heal my innermost hurts. I came to realize that the personality I had created over my lifetime was completely based upon service to other people. That is all I had ever known. The fact is, the only sense of belonging I had, stemmed from situations where I felt needed. While ever I was needed, I had no problem being the strong, capable one for other people to lean on. In time, I realized that it wasn't about what people said to me, or did to me. It was all about how my thoughts responded to those words and actions. It felt as if I was waking up from a long, long sleep and the waking was as painful as any birth.

The challenges … well, they were an essential part of unraveling and learning my life lessons. Somehow I knew that they were all part of God's grand plan. And even though I didn't completely understand, I trusted that everything was for a reason. No matter how big the challenge was, I knew God was not punishing me. Quite the contrary, I was being strengthened; I was growing new muscles to cope with life, and in doing so, learning to understand other people's suffering. Life has brought me so many challenges and so much change, that today I hardly recognize the person I used to be. I no longer live in the same world I did on the day when I wrote that mission statement. I am glad I did not listen to what other people said. If I had, I never would have dared. I never would have tried. I definitely would not be the person I am today!

I have learnt over the years that we should never take another person's opinion of our lives seriously. Don't allow another person's perception of you to limit the person you want to become. A friend of mine once said to me, 'Lesley, you get out and do things, while others sit back and think about it. If I told you there was something interesting at the end of the Amazon River, you would be off in your kayak and paddling.' And that's the absolute truth. To me, anything is possible and everything is probable. My understanding always comes as I question what I don't know, rather than going over what I do know. The speed at which our lives evolve can only be limited by our doubts about our ability to cope. It is our doubt that creates the negative energy and the testing of our belief in ourselves along the way. I have a saying: 'Let God's will be my will.' and that gives me the courage to keep going.

We are all developing the courage of our convictions. When you know what is right for you, when you no longer experience doubt, when commitment and faith meet; then, the heavens will move to bring you the opportunities you have been waiting for. A good example of fate in action is how I came to be in touch with Jenny B. all those years ago. Who would ever have thought being given a book could lead to a lifelong friendship! Today, I still count her as my friend, and I still think of her as a guiding light in the darkness of human chaos. She helped me to find my role—I see myself as a messenger who ignites the light of Spirit in this world and brings hope to others. My journey is about touching lives for a moment in time with a pure and gentle truth. In turn, those people go on to touch even more lives, and the transformation process continues. The earth's consciousness is moving forward. Caring and sharing the light of hope for over thirty years, Jenny B. no longer teaches spiritual development. Instead, she has put her knowledge and energy to use by becoming a very successful published author. I often wonder what would have become of my life if not for her.

The tiny seaside town near Coffs Harbour where we now lived was an idyllic place. It was absolutely perfect for any family wanting a healthy, quiet life. The town itself was a small close knit community. It was originally settled in the early 1800s for its timber, which was as valuable as the gold in the hills. Over time, farmers settled and townships sprang up. Large natural forests blanketed the mountain range which gently rose from a magnificent coastline of pristine waters and long, white deserted beaches. There was freshness and a cleanness to the air here that I had not felt before. Yes, I thought to myself, this was where our small family would find its home. I prayed life would be good.

CHAPTER FIVE

'To touch with love that holds no judgment.'

There were arguments and tantrums, and there was loneliness. I had many days when life just seemed too incomprehensible, too big, and too hard. At these times, my mind would end up screaming in frustration, 'I give up. I'm not going to try any more. It's too hard. I quit!' I didn't mean suicide; no, I meant that I would just stop trying to make everyone's world perfect. I was lucky in a way that Henry and I lived way out in the country. I didn't have the city's distractions; all I had was a lot of time, space, and an all pervasive aloneness. There were chores to do, a house to clean, paintings to paint, and children to tend to. I was the perfect wife—spotless house, baking done, meals prepared, children clean and tidy, chickens fed. I even found time to make a beautiful garden overflowing with flowers. But something was very wrong. One second I would be a cyclone of Mrs. Perfection. In the next, I'd be sobbing in the corner, trying to figure out what was missing in my life and what the heck was wrong. Life itself kept my feet firmly planted on the ground. Anger often flared, as family commitments stopped me from spending precious moments on searching out my secret passion. My husband, by this time, was quite beside himself; he spent more and more time at work, or off with his mates.

There was no doubt in my mind that Henry must have thought I had gone completely mad. I just could not settle; something was missing and I just had to find whatever it was. All Henry knew was that he was losing the girl he had married. She was changing and he was so frightened. His fears made him try harder to control me, and he was willing to do everything in his power to stop me. He didn't understand that the way to keep me was simply to love me. Instead, he became hard, nasty, and often abusive. His best weapon was emotional and mental cruelty, and his need to control loomed larger than life. Our marriage was in trouble. I was young and all I wanted was to be loved, but that sure was not happening in our house.

We moved constantly from place to place. We followed the work and there was a constant sense of being the drifters, never anchored to anywhere. We did see a lot of the country during those years though, and we learnt a lot about the practical skills of life as farmers and miners. We learned a lot about life, period! Finally, when we settled in our small coastal town, I thought for a moment that life would be ok, and that this might be what I had been missing. I wanted to find my purpose, beyond being a wife and a mother. I started work at the local hotel with my friend Rose. She was worried about me sitting at home all day, being depressed. So she spoke to her bosses and, before I knew it, I was working three or four evenings a week and the odd day shift on Saturday. I loved bar work, but not because of the normal reasons. It was a small country pub, and I just loved being busy and having something to do. Not only that, the money came in handy too. The money I earned provided me with independence, and that was a way to get to the next step in my life. Teaching meditation on a Sunday night wasn't enough. I wanted to understand more, so I would be able to reach more people. I wanted to learn how to become a therapist and maybe even go to university. Work for me was a means to an end, and my life was just beginning.

When I enrolled in a study course at the School of Natural Medicine to become a remedial massage therapist, war was officially declared in our marriage. Henry could not understand why there was a need to learn and become a little more independent. After all, isn't a woman's place in the home? All I wanted was for all our lives to be happier and to find a way to express myself. I honestly thought that finding my own strengths and career would surely be a help. Surely, following my passion for learning would help me find the missing pieces I needed to solve the puzzle. The study would challenge me, but it would also give me a sense of achievement and fulfillment which my heart so longed to experience. The sad thing was that there seemed to be no way to help Henry understand so he would give me the support I needed. There was so much soul-searching going on that, without realizing it, happiness began to drain away, leaving me even more miserable than before. I had become so consumed with finding myself that, without even realizing it, for a while I actually stopped living life. Spiritual awakening, or whatever you want to call it, had become an addiction—an addiction which would in the end cost me everything before I woke up.

I could tell you stories that would blow your mind. I could go on and on telling you about how I overcame my own fears and confusion. Life just kept happening; but with each challenge, I became a little more aware, a little more self-honest, and a little more courageous. I definitely became more determined to understand what life was about, and how to be aligned to my own true north.

By this time, my children were beginning to grow up and have their own issues to contend with. My eldest daughter was just about ready to leave home, one fledgling grown and independent. As she began to find her way in the world, I felt the pride that only a mother can feel. And Henry, well…he would rather be with his mates at the pub, or off fishing, than at home talking to me. Deep inside, I knew it didn't matter how hard I tried, or how pretty I looked. Nothing was going to get any better if I didn't find some answers. My sense of loss and confusion grew with each passing day, and the only thing that seemed to make sense in this crazy life was my interest in spirituality and healing.

My dreams were becoming even more intense. I dreamt of a slender man with sandy hair; full of passion, love, and intrigue. Each night he would visit in my dreams; his presence was so intense, so intimately sexual, that I would wake wondering if he was a ghostly love calling me across the dimensions of human time. Someone special was coming into my life; I could feel him calling me. His presence was as real as the grass beneath my feet and the sky above my head. Confusion reigned as this destined love from past life called me; taking hold of my body, mind, and soul.

Eleanor Roosevelt once said, 'Great minds discuss ideas; average minds discuss events; small minds discuss people.' Apparently I am a person whose brain likes to find new concepts. My idea was, that if human beings can get honest with themselves about their motivation and their actions, then surely life would have to improve. The law of attraction clearly states that like attracts like. So, if we have a flaw but are unable to see it, then that flaw will be presented to us in those around us, until we question if we ourselves behave that way. The law of attraction, I have discovered, works not only with positive attraction but also with negative. My quest to attain self-awareness had definitely become an obsession. I had no idea it had quietly taken over my life; I wanted to know it all, and I had to know it now! For a few precious fleeting moments everything about my life seemed so clear. Life was so simple; and then, as quickly as the realization hit, it totally disappeared. I had that déjà vu feeling and stood shaking my head in an attempt to clear the sensation which enveloped me.

Developing extra sensory perception is a natural evolutionary step. It's something that everyone on a spiritual path is drawn to pursue. In order to broaden our perception, we must first confront and heal our own issues. Changing on the inside is a prerequisite to anyone being able to consciously increase their sensitivity. If you don't heal and change, the subtle incoming information from natural guidance is just a mess of confused input. Like having a puzzle with a thousand pieces, that information is all jumbled up. To receive clear guidance and intuitive flashes, and be able to differentiate between it and mind chatter (ego), the seeker must cultivate a quiet mind. As we clear our own clutter and confusion, the mind becomes still. When the mind becomes still, the development of the sixth sense of perception is a natural result.

I felt like I had won the lottery. Yes! I had worked out one tinier piece of the puzzle. Meanwhile, I had been working as a barmaid and studying to get my Diploma of Remedial Therapies for about a year. I felt at home in the sleepy seaside town and had made friends with many of the local identities. One was Podge. You know, I can't remember his real name even now. He was just Podge because yes, he had a big round belly. Podge was a truck driver who came into the hotel for a beer every afternoon after work. What Podge really came in for was a chat about nothing in particular. All he needed was a friendly smiling face. I knew he had relatives living locally, and beyond that, it didn't matter to me what his history was. I took people how I found them, and he was always the perfect respectful gentleman. One day, Rose came into work looking a little stressed. 'Have you heard about Podge?' she said.

'No, what's happening? He hasn't been in for a while. What's going on?' I asked.

'Poor bugger has stomach cancer. It seems it's not good,' she said, shaking her head and looking so sad. We both had come to love this old man. He always had a smile and a tale to tell. And he always seemed to have a way of cheering up the afternoon. Days passed, and the news was that Podge wasn't going to get better. He seemed frail, and yet he never complained. One day, he just stopped coming in for his afternoon chat. So Rose and I decided we would go and see him and find out just what was happening.

Early one morning before work, we went to visit for a coffee. Podge looked so bad. He had begun losing weight, and it was obvious that he was in a lot of pain. We had a laugh and a joke, making small talk and avoiding the obvious. 'We wanted to come and see how you were getting along, and if you need anything,' Rosy said, squirming uncomfortably. 'You know you can count on us Podge, don't you,' she said as she leaned forward, putting a gentle hand on his shoulder. 'Maybe you should get Lesley to put her hot, healing hands on you. That might help,' she laughed. 'Seriously, her hands work wonders; take the pain right away, they do.' She continued, 'Anyway, it can't bloody hurt, that's for sure!' And so, I came to give Podge my first healing session. His swollen stomach looked so bloated and uncomfortable. I don't think any of us really thought anything would come of it, but to our astonishment—

something did … I closed my eyes and said a silent prayer for his pain to be lifted, and believe it or not, it was! I didn't know it at the time because all he said was how the heat coming from my hands felt good. He said he felt his body relaxing and the energy going right up and down his backbone. And that's how my healing work started, with my visits to Podge every couple of days. I somehow knew there was no cure physically for him, but in the days which followed, we chatted. He shared with me that more than anything, he wanted his broken relationship fixed before he passed.

The weeks kept rolling by, and I kept up with my visits. One day, as I was just ready to leave, Podge grabbed my hand, 'You know, Lesley, God could not have given me a better gift than you. I know I haven't told you, but when you put your hands on me, I don't have to have any morphine for at least eighteen hours—my pain goes away. I don't know how you do it, but it's always the same; the pain just goes.' My eyes filled with tears. How could this be? I felt so humbled and so privileged that I could do this for someone and that my prayers were being answered. Not only that, but in the last weeks of his life, Podge reconnected with his ex-wife and she was with him when he finally passed away. Some days, I still catch a glimpse of his old blue truck delivering a load of sand somewhere, and I smile. I know, he too watches over me, and my inexplicable love for an old man will stay with me forever.

That was to be the first of many experiences where healing came through my hands to bring relief to what was important. Healing is not always about the physical body; often it's about putting energy right, and about aligning those things which cause pain and suffering emotionally. Since that day, I have seen tumors vanish, frozen joints release instantaneously, relationships heal, and lives change in oh, so many ways. I had begun my apprenticeship; the road to becoming a healer was set, and there was no turning back, not ever. My intuition were about to show me so much about healing, health, and energy that my life was to become a constant adventure into a world that very few other people understood.

It was good to be living in a town with schools and shops where life was relatively normal. During the day, it bustled with activity. My favorite place was the beach; swimming in the surf was my number one pastime when I wasn't at work or running about after everyone in the family. I was no longer segregated and isolated but I did miss the peace of mind being in the bush brought to my soul. So, there were good and bad points, but life was evolving. My children were making friends, growing up, and finding their way in the world. It seemed as though we were in the right place. We had never been able to afford to buy a house; we had always lived in houses supplied by the properties we worked on. During those years, our wages were small, as deductions were made for having housing and meat supplied by the farmer. It was a different situation when renting. As wages increased, and now with us both working, we thought we could finally get ahead in the world. Maybe we could even buy a house in the future; who knew what might be possible. It seemed like there was something wrong but I couldn't work out what it was. I finally realized the more we earned, the more we spent. And as wages increased, the more money my husband thought there was to spend, the more the bills ran up.

We had stepped onto the empty pocket treadmill; it was going 'round and 'round and we weren't getting anywhere. I am not sure if it was just my husband's nature or if our relationship had something to do with it. I don't know exactly what the cause was, but he began drinking every day, and his drinking was something he was not willing or able to control. He said he just needed to relax, enjoy a beer, and be with his mates—fishing. I, on the other hand, had always dreamt of a life where my husband would want to share our life's experiences and spend time with me, helping to plan our future and wanting to own a home. Things just weren't working out; we were going in different directions with different goals, needs, and desires. The future was looking more and more precarious …

So, while we didn't own a home, we had lived in several; let me tell you about some of the strange experiences I have encountered in some I've lived in. Old homes are often filled with the ghosts of previous tenants; they leave their energy behind. If something powerful has happened there, the house can have what is called a residual haunting. This is like a tape playing over and over with the same activity recurring. The ghost can often be seen or heard by people, but it doesn't interact. A healer can release this energy and clear it. The other type of haunting is what is called an active haunting. In this situation, people who have passed over, constantly interact, or try to communicate with the living. I have found that old houses are often occupied by the people who built them, loved them, and had happy memories within them. Some occupants may even have passed over while living in their homes. In this case, it is as though the fabric of their lives binds their spirits to that space. It may also be that for some reason, they are unwilling to pass to the light where peace awaits them. In rare cases, it can happen that people die suddenly and become trapped in a reality where they have no awareness that they have died. Our house in Smith Street was no different. It was a big, old cumbersome house with verandahs; which, to make more space, had been converted to bedrooms. Downstairs had never been finished and upstairs, the wallpaper was peeling. I loved that old house. It had warmth to it, a feeling of safety and security. There, the spirit energies of past residents embraced our tiny family with love. Even though all my children actually saw the ghostly residents, no one was afraid of them. It was like having grandparents living with you but without the food bills.

At our Smith Street residence, the verandah looking north was my space. Here, the sun filtered in through the ancient jacaranda tree in the front yard. The tree had fine leaves of light green and around November, it would burst into a mass explosion of purple blossoms which would fill the air with sweet perfume. It was at this house that I began holding my weekly healing circle and personal development groups. People would just come. I have no idea how they found me or the group; people just turned up. I guess it was by word of mouth. The circle grew, and through this experience I was able to improve my skills at reading people, identifying their problems, and sharing the precious knowledge I had gathered.

It was around this time that something strange was happening; my life was strange anyway, but this was so strange I have never told anyone this part of my story … until now. I have to admit, it's a little confronting speaking about such intimate details, but …

During the night, or whenever I lay down to have a sleep, something, or someone would come and make passionate love to me. The power of sexual attraction was beyond anything I had encountered physically in my entire life. I could be sound asleep when I would feel the weight of someone moving onto the bed, encircling my body, dragging me down, and touching my skin in ways which set my whole body afire with need and desire. It was not a dream, I can say that definitely. What it was, I don't exactly know. But it felt as though a solid, physical ghost was taking me to the deepest, glorious, sacred places of 'passion never before encountered'.

Needless to say, these daily visits troubled me deeply. How could a spirit make love to someone alive? How was this possible? I had experienced hauntings before, but never any which crossed personal boundaries. The visits continued and although the mystery surrounding the visitations was concerning,

I had to admit, I began looking forward to going to sleep, so my 'mystery man' would come and take me to a world of such intense feelings of passion. Questions filled my mind: What was happening to me? Was this a real live person visiting me by way of astral projection?[8]

The answer that came back to me after asking that question was this: An unfulfilled love from another time was crossing the boundaries of space and time to be with me in this lifetime. I was

---

[8] Wikipedia: **Astral projection** (or astral travel) is an interpretation of **out-of-body experience** (OBE) that assumes the existence of an "**astral body**" separate from the **physical body** and capable of travelling outside it. Astral projection or travel denotes the astral body leaving the **physical body** to travel in an **astral plane**. The idea of astral travel is rooted in common worldwide religious accounts of the **afterlife** in which the consciousness' or soul's journey or "ascent" is described in such terms as "an... out-of body experience, wherein the spiritual traveler leaves the physical body and travels in his/her subtle body (or dream-body or astral body) into 'higher' realms."[1] It is frequently reported in association with dreams, drug experiences and forms of meditation. Patients have reported feelings similar to the descriptions of astral projection induced through various **hallucinogenic** and **hypnotic** (including **self-hypnotic**) means. There is no scientific evidence that there is any measurable manifestation of a consciousness or soul which is separate from **neural activity**, and there is no scientific evidence for the contention that one can consciously leave the body and make observations. Attempts to verify that such has occurred have consistently failed in spite of the variety of **pseudoscientific** claims to the contrary.

also shown that I would meet someone (a real person) significant and that meeting would change my life forever. Would it be for the better? That I didn't know; for you see, when something is karmic, spirit guides do not give you the full picture. If they did, it would interfere with your free will and therefore leave the lessons unfinished. So there was nothing I had to do, or could do, but to remain alert and wait for this 'real life' soul mate of mine to appear.

Some people only ever have relatives as guides; this could be their grandmother or someone who they have had a close physical association with. In my case, it was different. Since childhood, I seemed to have attracted guardians who all had one thing in common. I noticed that in my case, all had been powerful people who lived to protect the weak and bring a better way of life into this world. It was about this time that I became aware of a new spiritual guide, who I later came to know as Charlemagne.

One evening, I was feeling relaxed and just chilling out watching television when I felt this kind of electricity in the air. It felt as if someone was watching me; you know, those goosebumps you get, and that prickly feeling like someone's there. I turned to see who had come into the room. To my astonishment, in the corner of the room was an incredibly tall man wearing an ancient looking hooded cloak. Although his face was obscured by the hood, he didn't feel scary or bad. Instead, I was sensing he had something important to say to me. Without moving, I watched him for what seemed like a long time. He just stood with hands clasped together and head bowed slightly, as though he was waiting. I heard my own voice in my head say, 'Who are you and what do you want?' To my shock, I heard his reply, 'I am Charlemagne[9], once a great King of Avalon. I

---

[9] **Charlemagne**; King of the Franks from 768 to his death 814. He expanded the

have come to help you find both courage and answers.' With that, he raised his head and looked directly at me. His piercing eyes were so strong, so all knowing; I felt as though I had known this man forever.

He had the strongest face, like an old Viking King or Celtic man would have had. He wore a full beard, and his hair was a golden red blonde. His square-set jaw showed the muscles born of a difficult life. Obviously, he was a king in his own right—a timeless warrior and a knight of old. 'You remember then, how to talk without words,' he said. As his eyes met mine, I felt as though my mind were being swept back to another space and time. 'You do not need to speak. Your thoughts are enough,' he said. His lips did not move but his voice, like his face, was strong, and sweet like honey, 'We have reconnected now. I will never leave you. All you need to reach me are your thoughts. Take care, little one. Change is coming.' With that, in the blink of an eye, he was gone. I found myself shaking my head, wondering if I had just imagined the most bizarre but amazing thing of my life. How odd it all was, but how right it all felt. I felt as

---

Frankish kingdoms into a Frankish Empire that incorporated much of Western and Central Europe. During his reign, he conquered Italy and was crowned Imperator Augustus by Pope Leo III on 25 December 800, in an attempted revival of the Roman Empire in the West. Through his foreign conquests and internal reforms, Charlemagne helped define Western Europe and the Middle-Ages. His rule is also associated with the Carolingian Renaissance, a revival of art, religion, and culture. He also campaigned against the peoples to his east, especially the Saxons, and after a protracted war, subjected them to his rule. By converting them to Christianity, he integrated them into his realm and thus paved the way for the later Ottonian dynasty. He was smart, tough, aggressive and cunning. He was a great warrior, a brilliant general, very adept at diplomacy, skilled at earning loyalty from his people, and devoted to the welfare of his subjects. Charlemagne: a hard man -- but a great man.

though Charlemagne was a part of me, a part from somewhere back in the depths of history. I felt that he knew the answers to all the questions; not least, how to win the battle without bloodshed.

For many years from that day forward, Charlemagne was to become one of the main guiding influences in my life. His strength and wisdom always helped me to see the bigger picture and prompted me to question my emotional reactions to my circumstances. It was, I suppose, a very strange alliance; and yet, not. One of the understandings brought to me through his connection is that time is an illusion. Those we have known in other lifetimes and those we have been in other lifetimes, are still in existence. Death is not the end of life, it is only the beginning. All that we have known and been, stays connected to us; not just for this life, but for all lifetimes. We may draw upon other lifetimes; in fact, we do constantly draw upon other lifetimes in an attempt to progress as conscious souls. The intention of this progression is that one day we will finally understand and see the big picture of what life and reincarnation are all about.

CHAPTER SIX

'Never assume and never presume.'

I can't remember the day the phone call came, but I do remember the details. My friend Bob called me from town. He worked part-time in a bookshop and as a naturopath the rest of the time. Bob was excited on the phone, 'Lesley, I have someone here in the shop who I thought you might like to meet. He is a psychologist who is studying near-death experiences.' In his excitement, Bob's American drawl seemed to blur all the words together; he sounded so funny. He always reminded me of a cartoon character—full of fun and mischief. 'Can I put him on the phone? His name is ....' And before I had a chance to answer, a strange new voice spoke to me from a thousand years ago. It turned out, the professor was a psychologist from Sydney who was up this way to research near-death experiences (NDE) for his thesis, which was part of his qualifications. In his thesis, he hoped to establish the validity of the NDE. The professor was fascinated by people like me, who had actually experienced this. He had developed some sort of system whereby he asked questions, measured the variables in each case, and then correlated the responses to gain a totally impartial outcome. The professor asked if he could come to my home to interview me. Of course, I eagerly agreed. This was going to be something new—something exciting. Being interviewed about my strange life could bring me some answers; I hoped and prayed it would. Little did I know, that this meeting was about to unleash, not only the bringing together of two people in this lifetime, but a whole lot of unresolved stuff from centuries ago. My dream visitor had now become a living physical reality! Past was about to meet present, and the karma between us was just going to have to be cleared, one way or another.

A few days later, there was a knock at the door, and it was like, 'Oh, hello. It's so nice to meet you *again*.' My thoughts raced as his charisma swept me off my feet, but not his looks, for he was not overly handsome: 175cm, fit-looking, receding hairline, and a neatly-cut moustache. By all accounts, he was trying to be the professional, but we enjoyed each other's company so much that we couldn't help becoming best friends very quickly. He was in a long-distance relationship with a woman in Sydney, so I felt somewhat safe when having coffee or meeting him for lunch. At this time, there was no physical relationship, even though I have no doubt it was something we both wanted and longed for. I was married, and he respected my position, as any gentleman would.

Henry, however, didn't see things that way. Looking back, I am sure he thought I was having an affair because his behavior became much worse. The more alcohol my husband drank, the less I wanted to be around him; so my evenings were often spent out with the professor and his roommate. It drove Henry mad with jealousy. But in reality, all of us were just innocently whiling away the time with a glass of wine, a good discussion on spirituality, and everything that went with it. His imagination created something that was not physically happening. It's possible he was sensing the spirit visitor who was still coming to visit me regularly. It was the strangest, most unbelievable experience of my life, but I didn't want it to end. I didn't know the answer to that one. Things were happening in my life; I could sense that change was coming, but it wasn't of my doing this time.

I hungered for good company, for fun, for laughter, and to escape a hostile home environment. Henry wanted me back, but he had no idea how to get me back. His way was to bully me and embarrass me by making it look like everything was my fault. In his way of thinking, I should be the good woman, waiting for him with a clean house and a meal cooked, after his drinking binges or fishing trips. Somehow, in the midst of all this, my spirituality became my weapon. It was very wrong of me I know, but it's the only way I can explain it. I felt like I was defending my soul against evil: the evil of bullying, the evil of ignorance, and the evil of un-evolved thinking. It is strange but true—just how insidious spirituality can become if you fall into the trap. Without realizing it, my search for self-awareness and my hunger to find the answers had made my life a walking and breathing spiritual nightmare. I had learnt about the esoteric. I had learnt about the secret knowledge brought to my attention by my guardians. I had learnt about metaphysics*[10]. This hunger all but consumed my life and everyone in it.

---

[10] **Metaphysics** is a traditional branch of philosophy concerned with explaining the fundamental nature of being and the world, although the term is not easily defined. Traditionally, metaphysics attempts to answer two basic questions in the broadest possible terms. 1. What is ultimately there? 2. What is it like?

An outcome of the all-consuming hunger was that I monitored, examined, meditated, diarized, and dissected every part of my life. I made sure everything was in its place, and there was a place for everything. I used to think that if I could keep everything in its right order, then, God willing, life would have to work. The harder I tried the more energy and thought it took to keep it all in place, and the wearier I became. It was a cycle of repeating ups and downs. There was pain and there was anger; at times there was self doubt. But my suffering drove me onwards and I dug deep within to find the strength and determination to overcome every obstacle in my path. The need for inner fulfillment became the ultimate compelling drive within me, and that gave me the courage to move onwards, no matter what the odds were.

There were many happy times in our marriage, in spite of all the chaos inside me. These days, I tend to think more of the happy times and wonder, if I were then, the person I have now become, would our marriage have worked out? Would we still be married? I was far from perfect; I was immature, and at times a plain spoilt brat. He was just being who he was; so sadly, we both ended up losing out. Happy times for us were fishing with the kids, barbeques, and family adventures. It's sad that so much of that gets forgotten. For him, these days there is nothing but hatred for me. But deep inside, I know that is simply his way of still loving me. It took time for the marriage to break down due to irreconcilable differences.

Henry announced he was leaving me and our son James would go with him. A boy needed his father so I just stepped back and let it happen. Although now, when I look back, I think how petty all the arguments had been, we could have changed it, and so much of what happened was based upon both of our immaturity and stupidity. We both needed to grow up and lean to deal with the emotional baggage we were carrying around. I was lonely and wanted to feel appreciated. He couldn't deal with emotions so he spent every waking moment either at work, or fishing. Being so angry with someone that you could hurt them is no way to live. Henry left, taking my son with him, and that was the end of that. I missed my son desperately, but I had this stupid belief that a son needs his father, so I didn't interfere. I had no idea how I was going to survive financially, I just had faith that somehow I would.

It wasn't long before the energy in my life began to change. It was full-on growing time. I was now a qualified therapist. I also ran healing circles each week, at which people would come to sit and meditate, learn about healing, and share their thoughts on all things spiritual. After twenty-five years of marriage, I was left with just 75 dollars in total, to my name. While there were no debts, there was no money for anything, and this was very limiting. Perhaps to escape my plight, I found myself daydreaming of travel destinations. London, Europe, and Canada were on my bucket list. I had always wanted to go to Vancouver, where my eldest brother lived, but I'd never had the money or the opportunity to go.

For a while, my search turned outward as I worked, and tried to find satisfaction and fulfillment in the outside material world. I thought money would ease the pain—home, new clothes, travel, fine-dining—everything at my fingertips. Eventually however, I just had to come down to earth and realize that the emptiness in my life was not anyone else's fault but mine. I had to find a way of being responsible and waking up to what I was doing that was causing me the struggle and the pain. The stupid thing is, I was so entrenched in finding answers that I could not see, 'that very thing' was the cause of the problem. My desperate search for whatever it was I was looking for, had caused me to throw away the very thing that was most important in my world—my family. I mistakenly thought I had to leave the town that I loved and move on. I thought I would be better off without my husband, and I felt my children no longer needed an overprotective mother. In hindsight, I wish someone had told me to wake up at that point. I wish I had known how to reach out to my husband and fix all the things which drove us apart. After all, I did love him, I just didn't like him. All the wishing in the world was definitely not going to put this problem right. My mother used to say, 'If wishes were horses, beggars would ride. If turnips were watches, I would wear one by my side.' I can hear her now, 'Don't go wishing your life away my girl, live now!'

All was not lost however; for I was growing and learning about myself. I was learning who I was and how to be more true to being that person. In the process, I was clearing away my confusion, to reveal what the essential ingredients of life were. I was discovering the truth about what makes life peaceful, and what makes us feel as though we are fulfilling the grand picture we were born to create.

One evening, I was standing at the sink peeling potatoes. My mind was kind of blank; you know, like you feel when you are daydreaming. All of a sudden, I heard the voice of Charlemagne, my guide. The voice was so strong and clear that it was just as though someone was speaking into my right ear, 'Get your passport; you're going to Canada.' I got such a fright that I jumped, and dropped the potato knife in the sink. I thought I must be going mad. Yea, right! Me going to Canada! And how do you think I'm going to do that? I thought to myself. So I ignored the voice, and life kept on. About two weeks later, I was again peeling potatoes at the sink when I heard Charlemagne's voice and again he said, 'Get your passport; you're going to Canada.' I recall it as though it were yesterday.

I calmly leaned on the kitchen sink. Then I looked up in the air as though I were speaking to someone up there, and I answered, 'Well, ok then, I will get my passport. But you'll have to fix it for me to go, because I sure as hell can't!' The very next day, feeling very stupid, I trotted off to the post office to put in an application for an Australian passport. It was an act of faith by all accounts, but it sounds absolutely like an act of stupidity. I walked out of the post office, having spent the only money I had on a passport. I just shook my head and kept on walking across the street to my car. 'Well, I have done it,' I spoke out loud to no one there.

I was now forty-two years old and on my own. For the first time in my life, since the age of fifteen, I had no responsibility for others. I loved being single and not having to do anything for anyone. My meditation classes were growing in popularity. My clinic was steadily busy, although not a huge amount of money was coming in. Life was good! It was calm for the first time in many years. The professor and I had started casual dating. It was going well; he was funny, charismatic, worldly and exciting. He rode a BMW motorbike and I absolutely loved to go out riding the highways with him. Fate seemed to have lined up all the ducks in a row. This turned out to be better than I could have imagined, for my life was being governed by a much higher purpose now, and I had no idea that my spirit visitor had been working miracles in the background. A huge surprise was about to fall from the sky, bringing the professor and me even closer together.

The professor was an amazingly seductive man, something my poor husband had not been. He had a way of keeping himself just out of heart's reach which made him irresistible. When his fingers ran down my back it would be like a million volts of electricity coursing through my veins. His touch was tantalizing, exhilarating, and euphoric. His manner of making everything seem more alive kept drawing me into his web, just like a moth headed for a sticky death trap on a moonlit night. Our love was young; everything seemed so vibrant, something I had not had the chance to feel before in my life. The fact that I had married so young had robbed me of so many life experiences. It was now my time and I would be dammed if I would worry about the wagging tongues and the nosy Parkers in my hometown. People are always so quick to judge; and yet, mostly they have far worse skeletons in their own cupboards.

My eldest brother lived in Canada, but I had never had contact with him, not ever! He would call my mother once in a while but he never bothered with any of his siblings. He had never phoned me or written to me. I remember seeing him only three times in forty years and that was on the rare occasions when he visited Mum and Dad. He was a stranger in reality, just linked by blood. It was about 9 pm on a Saturday evening when the phone rang and to my shock, the call was from my long-lost big brother, 'Hey, Lesley, how are you doing? I hear you have been having a hard time of it lately, and you could do with a holiday. How would you like to come to Vancouver and stay with your sister-in-law while I go overseas for work?' Well, I nearly dropped the phone. I could not believe it, a trip to Vancouver! My brother kindly paid for my ticket, and all I needed to do was to have some spending money for food and whatever else I needed. I couldn't wait to get on the plane!

That night, the professor came to dinner and I excitedly told him about my brother's offer. He looked at me, stunned. 'I'm planning a trip to the USA in February to see some friends; I go every year. What about we travel together?' he grinned. Well, my heart raced—a trip of a lifetime with the man of my dreams! What more could a girl want! He continued, 'We can make it fun—stop in San Francisco, get a car, drive to the Grand Canyon, see a few places, and then go on to Vancouver. From there, I can get a car and drive down to Seattle to see Mick.' We both were so excited. Life was good and it seemed everything was falling into place. My life was changing; I was finally being presented with the opportunity to grow, travel and gain some of that worldly experience. At the time, I thought all I wanted was to leave the years of unhappiness behind and forget it all. What I didn't realize was that I was leaving behind a large part of who I was, and that the girl who married the boy from up the street, the girl who was the mother of my children, would not be returning with me. Without realizing it, I had abandoned the most important part of my life—my children who had taught me so much and made my life something of a magnificent tapestry.

At that time, I believed 100 per cent that I would be guided in my journey to find my life's purpose; and that no matter what happened in my life, there was a reason for it to happen. On 19 February 1991 we boarded the plane and off we flew on a grand adventure. I was finally going to see America and Vancouver. I felt so excited that I thought I could burst! We had been flying about twelve hours when the captain's voice came over the loudspeaker, 'Sorry, folks, we are being diverted to Hawaii. One of our passengers has suffered a heart attack and we just can't risk continuing on to LA. It will be necessary for everyone to clear customs in Hawaii; then a shuttle bus will pick everyone up and you will be taken to a hotel. Unfortunately, we cannot continue on tonight, but another flight will take you to LA International at 8.30 tomorrow morning.'

Ah well, the professor said it didn't matter. We would just be late picking up the rental car, and that was no big deal. So we settled in for the evening with a late supper in our hotel in beautiful Honolulu; it was my first night on foreign soil since the age of four years old. It must have been about 2.30 am when I woke. I felt quite odd, as though I had electric energy flowing all over me and through me. Abuzz-like tingle filled every part of me. The professor was sleeping soundly beside me in the king-size bed. He looked fine and didn't seem to be aware of the strange magnetic glow filling the large room. I tried to sleep, closing my eyes, but the energy was getting stronger and stronger.

Rolling over onto my back, I opened my eyes to see that the room was full of a strange blue light. I couldn't believe what I was seeing. Straight up towards the ceiling, floating above me and facing me, was the most beautiful woman I had ever seen. I blinked once, twice, and three times but she was still there. I was mesmerized. Whoever she was, she had her eyes closed, as if she was asleep. She had the most beautiful milk-white skin and very long blonde hair. On her head, she wore a skull cap of pearls—tiny, intricate, glistening pearls. It reminded me of something a bride would have worn on her wedding day, perhaps back in the sixteenth century in Arthurian times. Her gown of finely woven cotton or silk also looked like something that had just stepped out of King Arthur's time. All I could think was how absolutely amazing she looked. I watched as the energy ran in shafts of colored light between our two bodies. It was like the ribbons of light that make up the northern lights (the aurora borealis) but close up it was so spectacular. As the energy grew, I felt as though I was being connected with, or locked into an energy grid with this beautiful spirit visitor. Somehow we had merged and I instinctively knew we were the same spirit—we were one. With that, it was as though someone had waved a magic wand over me, for I fell back into sleep; and it was the deepest, most profoundly peaceful sleep I had experienced in years. Although I had no idea what was happening at the time, I have since been given an explanation by my guides. I was told that this merging of energy occurred because I had apparently healed enough of my life, that I was ready to take on re-awakening another dimension of myself. I could then begin to heal it also. This was really quite extraordinary!

Getting back to my everyday reality, there were so many questions and right now, no answers. I had fallen deeply in love with the professor; I had not held back. I wanted him to want me as much as I wanted him—spiritually, mentally, physically, and emotionally. I had no idea of who he was and that he was really a wolf in sheep's clothing who had come to teach me one of the darkest, deepest lessons of my life. The signs were all there: the control, the need to dominate, the need to be secretive. But a woman blinded by love sees nothing of the reality, only the illusion. The professor was the master of illusion. He showed everyone what he wanted them to see. Only behind closed doors, did the devil himself show his face. I was about to learn one hell of a lesson. Although I didn't realize it, fate was lining me up for the biggest whammy wake-up call of all.

Our trip to Vancouver had been fantastic. Not everything was perfect, but we had many wonderful memories. There was so much that was new and exciting happening between us, that I trusted life was going to continue to bring us even closer together; or so I thought. The first real sign of problems in our relationship came on our return. The professor hated my children; he hated my children with a passion. He wanted me, 'not my brats', as he put it. The punishment for arguing my stand was that he banned my children from ever stepping foot into his house. This tore me apart. Here was a man who I respected and had fallen in love with, with all my heart, and he was tearing my heart apart. My children had been my life up until this point. I didn't know what to do, so I set about trying to fix it. The harder I tried, the worse things became. Although the professor had a daughter, he had never really been a father to her. He didn't know what teenage kids could be like, or what having grandchildren around was like. All he knew was what he knew, and he wasn't willing to give an inch. Needless to say, our relationship started to fall apart, and within two years I had become anorexic and a nervous wreck. Little by little, things were coming out about the true nature of the professor and what he thought about our relationship. I asked my God, 'Why did you bring me into this situation? What am I supposed to learn?' Silence was their response.

Looking back, I knew what was going on. The professor had many women, all over the world. They all believed he was their man, that he loved only them. None of that mattered to me; the moment he took me in his arms I was helpless to his charms. My addiction to him began to spiral out of control. I wanted only him. We lived together, but that was all; there were clear boundaries in our relationship. There were no niceties such as the sharing of finances or possessions; what was his was his, and what meager possessions were mine, were also his. There would be no negotiation on his part. If I wanted to be in his life, it would have to be on his terms; I could either take it, or leave it.

I questioned our relationship; why did it have to be this way? If this man were my soulmate, shouldn't things be different than this? My mind was working overtime. My brain chatter was in a state of chaos. But I was in love, and I wasn't about to pay attention to it, or to anything else. It's a hard thing when you love someone who doesn't accept who you are with all your trappings. That is a lesson I was about to learn. Life with the professor was about to become a confusing battleground, much worse than anything I had ever experienced with my husband. I was about to find out there was much more to the man than I ever dreamt possible. His problems were far worse than anything I had ever encountered. But I was in love, and as we all know, love makes fools of even the bravest and most intelligent of people.

You might at this point wonder how a spiritually aware woman, in possession of powerful intuition, could end up in such a mess. Well, I am embarrassed to say, I may have been meditating and doing all the right things, but I just wasn't listening very well. The warning signs were there but I didn't want to notice them. My intuition was trying to make me aware of the signs. God knows, I was being confronted by the horrible truth every day! I just refused to acknowledge that this man had his own agenda and I, and my family, was in fact no part of it. I was hanging on to what I thought was love, hanging on with both hands and my heart wide open.

I didn't want to listen to the rumors and my own gut feelings about the other women in his life. The professor was always so secretive; meetings with his ladies, lunches, holidays overseas, and phone calls continued behind my back. I was definitely going through a huge state of denial. I resolved that I would fix the problems in my life by becoming the woman he wanted me to be. My prayer was, he would choose me over the others. I thought, if I could be perfect by trying my best to make sure he was happy and content, then … Now, who was I kidding? I kept getting intuitive flashes. I kept seeing the warning signs. Deep down I knew, and all the meditation in the world was not about to save me from the grief and heartache of the next few years.

I was complacent in the fact that I knew things weren't right, and yet I stubbornly continued anyway. For one thing, the professor had me tied in knots about eating. I lost so much weight that I could wear size 10 clothes and weighed in at 68 kg, 10 kg less than my normal weight. He insisted on me wearing clothes he liked, never showing my legs, and always being careful not to show any cleavage. Oh, and wearing swimmers around other men … My heavens! He never would speak to me again. I have to laugh when I think about what I put myself through.

All the time, I kept thinking I just wasn't good enough and kept on feeling the pain. I witnessed violent outbursts of temper, like the time he smeared a hot dog all over a car windscreen at Wal-Mart in the USA because the man had stolen his parking space. That black, seething mass of temper would come to the surface whenever things didn't go his way. I learned fast to shut my mouth and become invisible. Why I put up with it, I have no idea! Maybe I didn't really know what love was. Maybe I had to find out where my own thinking was flawed in me feeling I was lesser a person? It didn't matter really, because this new wonderful relationship was headed for a brick wall at a hundred miles an hour.

It all came to a head late one evening. We had just returned from our annual holiday and I was in the bedroom, getting ready for bed. I can't even remember what I said but it was something quite insignificant; and I was understandably shocked when, in the next moment, his hand connected with my face and down I went. The shock had a bigger impact than anything I had ever experienced with my husband. My husband never hit me. 'Men don't hit women,' he would say. By the time the professor stopped, he was crying. He sobbed and sobbed, but that didn't help me, for sure.

'You made me do that! Why did you make me do that?' he blurted out. I felt my heart shatter into a million pieces. This was not the man I fell in love with. What the professor was in fact, was a street angel and a house devil, and I had locked myself in his cage. I had no money, he saw to that. Every penny went into running the house he owned. And so, there was no means of escape. I had become the woman who loved too much. I found myself caught in the ultimate trap of loving someone so much that I sacrificed myself for that love. Over the next months, we tried to work things out. The professor told me how his father had been a boxer and beat his mother constantly. There were tragic stories about how he hid under the kitchen table and watched his mother being dragged around the kitchen by her hair. My heart went out to this man. Maybe he could get help. And maybe he could fix this; he did not need to be his father's son.

At this point I began doing some detective work of my own. I knew a couple of people who had connections with a few of his past ladies. I contacted the ladies, asking for advice and gingerly broached the subject of his behavior. 'He is always like that,' one woman said. 'Get out of there, he won't change.' These were her words of warning to me. Undeterred, I thought I could fix him. I was sure I could get him to get help. How misguided can a well-meaning woman in love be! Away from home, he was the charming, wonderful man who solved everyone's problems. At home, he was someone who could drop the charade any time he wanted, and turn into the ugly, angry, violent thing which nightmares are made of. I was never a person to give up, and so this horrid, dysfunctional relationship was bound to keep on its course until I realized one important thing. During those years, I did see a psychiatrist who was a close friend, and he helped me. He had it all on record; he saw the bruises hidden beneath the clothes and the wounds as they appeared on my soul. The look of compassion in his eyes made me feel like a very stupid woman indeed. I felt so ashamed to admit being a battered wife or partner, whichever you want to call it. What was this thing I had been caught up in? Why couldn't I walk away? What did I need to learn from this? So many questions and not enough answers.

Life went on and the years came and went, until one day, the final confrontation twigged my brain into understanding what this whole nightmare was about. We had just come back from another trip to the USA. The trip had been a bit delicate, with the Professor having several of his hissy fits during the six week visit. He never hit me while we were away but the yelling and screaming, and the disgusting words that spilled out of his mouth at times, were more than anyone should have to endure. During our trip we had made a special trip to Carolina to meet with Dr. Ian Stevenson, the great specialist on reincarnation. The trip went well, but not as the professor expected. Dr. Stevenson was a wonderfully dapper man who was wearing a neat white suit and two-tone shoes when we met. He was amazingly charming as well, and welcomed us with open arms. But the funny thing was, he was more interested in speaking with me, than he was in speaking with the professor, and that didn't go down too well. That evening, we decided to celebrate being home by going out to dinner and a movie. The night was cool, the mood was light, and I was glad to be back on Australian soil. We had enjoyed a nice evening and had just arrived home when the conversation turned to a discussion about spirituality. 'It's not right, the fact that you see so much and know so much, when I'm the one with the Ph.D.,' the words spat out like shards of glass in my direction. 'You are nothing! You are no one! I should be the one getting the recognition not you!'

That night, I made a pact with God, 'God, you get me through tonight without being bashed, and I promise I will leave. I promise, God, just get me through tonight.' And God did. The next morning, the professor went to work as if nothing had happened. The moment he drove out of the apartment block, I became a woman on a mission. I ran around the house like a mad woman, collecting all my things and throwing them in the back of my little old car. Having done that, I stood at the door, took one last look, and tossed the key inside. I was closing the door on that part of my life.

No going back, no explanations, I was out of there as fast as my car would take me. I had just enough money to get to my sister's house in Brisbane, where I knew I would be safe. Thank God, I finally listened! I don't know if I would be alive today if I had not finally realized there was nothing wrong with me—it was his problem. I actually had reached the point where I could no longer put myself in a harmful situation, simply because I loved him. I learnt the lesson that my higher self had been trying to get me to understand, I had learned to value myself and trust myself.

Another chapter of my life had closed. I now understood what abused people experienced. I understood the traps of love, and because of this, I would ultimately help others heal their scars and become free from their pain. It's easy to say I should have paid attention to my intuition. But at the time, I was a woman in love who was in denial and just didn't listen: not to my intuition, not to my friends, and not to my family. Moral of the story: the universe was teaching me about loving myself more than being the object of another person's love, no matter how warped that might have been. The hard fact was, I had always sacrificed myself in the name of love, and my spirit guardians were attempting to help me break that cycle of destruction.

The professor and I were in a relationship for about four years. Living with someone who was psychotic was just about the worst thing I could have experienced. In the end, the only one who could save me from this living hell was me. I found my courage that day, and ran from the relationship. Once again, I was down to a couple of boxes of possessions. My sister is a very creative woman, quiet and intuitive. I didn't want to be a burden to her so I thought about how I could start my own business. Maybe I could do spiritual readings, hands-on healing, and use my remedial therapies with people. Suddenly, life opened up new possibilities and probabilities for me. Before too long, I was making enough money to get by. When I wasn't working, I continued to study parapsychology, healing, and energy. I learned how the body templates worked and how the aura reveals a person's emotions, health, and illness. I learnt to recognize a holistic picture of a person and their life, simply by focusing my attention and switching my thinking to another level. People thought I was spooky in that, I just knew stuff; but to me, it felt totally normal. As for me, I believed that everyone could do what I was able to do if they had the patience and perseverance to devote to understanding energy. I learnt to trust my senses; there was no other way. I wanted so much to use my skills to help people and I found that those who needed me just seemed to find me and reach out to me. Sometimes, this was via the most bizarre pathways. I could meet a stranger in a shop and in five minutes they would be telling me their life story. They would then look at me strangely and say, 'Why on earth did I tell you that!' Children would seek me out, frequently pulling away from their mother's hands, running to me, and then giggling as if they had found something precious. It was quite odd, come to think of it. But then, what was normal? The questions continued to flood my mind.

My sister's old house was home. In part, it was nearly falling down, but it was home. I settled into the spare room and the sense of family held me together emotionally. My children were either married or working so they no longer needed me. My nerves were by now shot to pieces as a result of my dramatic few years with the professor, and my self-confidence was shattered into a million pieces. My big question was, if spirituality was supposed to heal your life, then why was it that I moved from one disaster to the next? Looking back over my life, it hadn't been getting better; it just kept getting worse and worse! I hadn't yet realized, in order for my life to be healed, it would first have to be broken apart by experiences that would address flaws in my thinking. God would strip me bare to the bone before this journey was finished.

Awakening is a painful process. Becoming conscious of how we have played the game of life and, in doing so, created our own worst nightmares, is a huge piece of the lesson being dealt us. I had learnt much up to this point in my life, and no doubt I will still be learning up until the day I shuffle off my mortal coil. So now, it was time to look at my fears square in the eye and get on with it. For each of us, our life is the centre of our universe. The word *universe* means one song. So, in fact, we are the centre of our one song. We will one day sing in harmony with all other living beings; that's the plan anyway. When life is fine and all rose-colored glasses, we don't bother to question or search. Mediocre day-to-day existence has nothing within its structure to provoke change. Pain, especially the pain associated with love, is the greatest tool God (or Universal Consciousness) has to prod us to grow. I was once told there are three ways to enlightenment. The first is through suffering, and we all know that one well. The second is through acceptance; that is, when you know there must be a reason for what is happening to you, but you just don't know what that reason is. The third way to enlightenment is through purpose—a soul with purpose is unstoppable!

I had been living with my sister for about six months. Life had regained some sort of balance and I felt well again. I could sense that change was in the air once more, as I had been having dreams in which I was dressed in a suit and sitting in an office, looking very professional. The signs were there that it was time for the next evolutionary step. I was sitting in a coffee shop when the call came. It was Michael, 'Lesley, are you doing anything at the moment? I have the perfect job for you. Are you interested?'

'You know me Michael, always on for a challenge,' I replied enthusiastically. 'When can we meet?' The time was set, the interview held, and before I knew it, my life had switched gears again. I was off to live in sunny Queensland on the Gold Coast, where I had secured a good paying position. I would be running a pilot employment program for people who were long-term unemployed. I had met Michael some years before and he knew of my abilities to read people and to help them find their way in life. I certainly wasn't going to say no to that. I had been to see my new office and it was fine, but my search for an apartment was not quite so easy.

I had looked all day at rental properties in the paper, but nothing had that 'This is the place.' feel about it and I was running out of options. I was beginning to feel downhearted. The last tiny flat I had looked at, had a landlady who I had no doubt would be the landlady from hell. I politely left, hopping back behind the driver's wheel of my old car. I was exhausted so I sat back, closed my eyes, and wondered where my next home would be. I certainly knew what I didn't want, I thought to myself. And, right at that moment, I heard the words loud and clear in my right ear, as though someone were sitting next to me, 'Well, what do you want?' I was shocked by this sudden intrusion into my thoughts, but I was equally shocked that I spoke out loud, and without hesitation, in reply to a voice that I took to be Charlemagne's, 'I want a place high on a hill that looks out over the sea. I don't care if I have no furniture; I want to see the sea.' And with that, I started the old white car and drove off down the road towards the small seaside town of Tweed Heads. I had no idea where I was going, but I felt as if I was being shown the way. Ah, another real estate office. Ok, what about this one? I stopped the car and walked in, addressing the young woman behind the counter, 'I'm looking for somewhere to live, and overlooking the sea. Do you have anything?'

She smiled up at me, 'Yes, we do actually. We have this apartment. It's been empty six weeks, and I have no idea why. It's such a lovely place. Do you want the key to have a look?' I didn't hesitate, of course. She passed me the key and gave me the address. Once again, I hopped in my car and drove up the hill, this time with a sense of enthusiasm in my heart. I stopped at the front of a large white apartment building and opened the gate. The key fitted the main entrance door, so I went up the stairs and opened the door to the apartment. Well, I was home! I felt it right to the very core of my soul. I didn't even look at the whole apartment. I stood in the entrance way and the feeling just washed over me, and I knew. I closed the door and within half an hour had signed the lease. I had found my new home!

The unit was big, too big for just me really, but I didn't care. It had five walls of glass looking to the sea. The building was shaped like a honeycomb, so my lounge room, kitchen, dining room, and bedrooms all looked out to sea. Large glass windows with no fly screens slid back to expose the whole unit to the elements of nature.

This was to be my home for the next year; I loved every second that I lived there. The sounds of the sea brought peace to my heart, and even though my health was about to take a nose dive, nothing else really mattered anymore. I had a home and it was mine. I purchased a bed and a refrigerator. Another friend loaned me an old lounge, a coffee table, and a TV. Life was good and, for the first time, totally uncomplicated. I had room to breathe, room to heal, and room to find out a little more about whom I was, and what it was I had come into this life to finish.

It was 1994. I had come so far, but somehow not much had changed. I loved my job, and I loved working with the people I had taken under my wing to help. I still kept up my spiritual work by attending expos and conducting spiritual consultations; and I have to say, I became very proficient at psychic readings, even managing to help out in a few missing people's cases. But, it was still not enough to fulfill me. There was something else I wanted to do. Back in the days when I was married, I began to write a book as a way of processing my thoughts and resolving my issues. Writing for me, had become a habit, a part of my daily routine. I now had the time to devote to this task; I made up my mind that I would finish the book I had started. Determined to learn how to tell a story in a way which would inspire and capture the hearts of those who opened its cover, I would write, rewrite, and rewrite again. I had never been known to give up; it was not in my nature to do that.

Today was like any other day. With a cup of tea in hand and my trusty computer turned on, I settled back and prepared myself mentally to write. My mind was a whirlwind of thoughts and ideas; ready to pour forth into that magical machine we call 'the computer'. The next chapters of the manuscript were taking shape in my mind and the words were pushing and shoving to be expelled onto the paper. The day's writing was about to begin.

To gain a clearer perspective on my thoughts, I found it helpful to begin the day by recording the words on a tape recorder and then transcribing them sometime later. By listening to my thoughts over and over, it was easier for me to see subtle aspects of meaning that might require a little more explanation or an extra word here or there. Eventually, I would be satisfied with the wording of a passage—the whole thing transformed and springing to life, like a magical movie script created before my eyes. That's what I was doing when ...

At that moment, my attention was stolen away by the first brilliant rays of the sun's light bursting forth in a cascade of golden beams over the horizon. I loved to watch the sunrise over the sea. It was and still is the most awesome sight—an inspiration of life renewing itself. First light of dawn brings with it the most incredible sense of being part of the splendor of life. I felt blessed with the gift of watching the majesty of the universe unfold for another day. The dark sea was beginning to come to life. Colors changed as the sun's reflection danced through the waves, merged with the flooding white froth, and caressed the rock wall beneath my window. Off in the distance, I could hear the drone of diesel engines as the fishing trawlers moved slowly up the Tweed River. The tide was just right for them to cross the bar, and I imagined the busy deckhands as they prepared for the day ahead. I watched a flock of hungry gulls that flew in circles, squawking and screeching, as they followed the straggling team of tiny boats out to sea.

What a beautiful place I lived in! I didn't have much furniture, but I could see the sea. My life was being guided; people who needed me seemed to find me, even though I had no idea how they did. I put it down to synergy or synchronicity; they knew someone, who knew someone else, who spoke to someone, who had heard of me. I seemed to somehow reset people's start buttons and get them back on track with what I did to help them. My thoughts turned to my clients, who I would be working with later that day. I had found that they were often damaged by life, and damaged by the narrowness of their thinking. They were damaged by the limitations of thinking that what they were taught was true; when in fact, it wasn't. I saw people damaged by trying to force themselves into moulds created by society, moulds which (in the eyes of the great sculptor, God) were flawed beyond repair. It struck me how everyone is different in some ways; yet, everyone is the same in others. We all have the same human needs to be cared for, to love and to be loved. Once again, the computer screen grabbed my attention.

'All right, time to work,' I muttered to myself. For just a moment, I wondered if this story was ever going to be finished. 'Probably not,' I surmised 'A work in progress ... Yes, that's it, life is a work in progress!' I struggled with my old, maroon dressing gown, arranging it comfortably to cover my bare legs. The day's writing began to flow from me, and I began to read out loud the already completed pages of the manuscript.

As I began to read, the strangest thing happened from the moment my words first broke the stillness of the morning air. You see, the universe gave me quite a challenge when I was born dyslexic. Words defied my determination and intention to write them coherently; words challenged me, eluded me, and turned my head into jelly. I'm understating the facts when I say that as an adult, I didn't always get the words right the first time. As a child, my dyslexia meant that I had to find other ways to express myself.

I drew upon my creative talents instead, and learnt to express myself by drawing pictures when I wanted to say something, and painting pictures to express how I felt about the beauty that surrounded me. This became a real strength for me, to the point where I developed a real desire and drive to find a way to create pictures with words. It must have worked because my strength in this area was confirmed when I once did one of those psychological assessments, the type that tells you what job you are best suited for. My scores were Entrepreneur (98%), Leader (99%), Self-motivated (98%), and Creative Asset ('Visual Linguist'). We all have gifts, precious and rare; writing and understanding people are mine. Once I found out I could write (And the funny thing was, this was a complete turnaround from my childhood.), I wanted to combine this skill with my passion to eliminate suffering in people's lives (including my own). There was then one huge push to go against the odds (of my dyslexia) and find a way. Don't think for a minute that it was easy. It took a lot of hard work and as well as that; the challenge for me was to believe in myself and just do it.

I continued to work on my manuscript, deep in thought. While my writing was progressing, my days were much the same … Not for one minute did I ever think life would be like this! I had been searching for the answer for so long. And I was so tired—tired of the searching, tired of the self-doubt, and tired of the loneliness. The feeling of not belonging anywhere persisted, the enduring peace I sought still eluded me, and my life seemed to go from one catastrophe to another. Relationships came and went. Physical things brought only temporary contentment. I wanted more. I felt as though there was someone else I would rather be, and some other life I would rather live. But in truth, I was stuck in mine. How on earth was I going to get from here to there? Where was 'there' anyhow?

This is when I discovered that a part of finding your way, is finding out what you don't like. Sometimes you have to experience many things in order to discover the simple truth about what makes you happy. There is no other way. The truth about human nature is, a goal will only be achieved if it is respected 100 per cent. And, you have to respect where that goal is coming from (yourself) in order to achieve it. So, the essential ingredient in achieving your potential is self-respect. You must become a person you can respect by adding qualities to your life like honesty, integrity, and courage. If you don't respect yourself, then life will always be difficult.

I never used to respect myself. I felt guilt, and pain, and anger, and I couldn't shake them off. They ate away at me every day with thoughts like, why couldn't I make my marriage work? Why did I fail at being a wife? Why was I such a cranky, angry mother to my children, who I loved more than life itself? Why was life so hard? Why didn't people like me and want to be my friend? I had all this stuff flying around in my head every day—guilt, blame, anger, resentment, jealousy, and envy—all talking at me at the same time. I had the seven deadly sins, all right; and they were all happening at once! They just kept oozing out of every pore of my being, and nothing helped to ease the pain. I was lonely and missing the one constant that had been with me most of my life. I was missing family, a husband, and a sense of belonging somewhere. I wanted my soulmate to find me, to rescue me, and to take me home. I just wanted to be happy. Was that so much to ask!

I meditated, I read books, and I did everything possible to improve my life. No matter what happened, I tried so hard not to be angry. I tried, and tried, and then tried some more. I tried to be beautiful. Men were attracted to me. It was like I was a bright fire fly; so many kept seeing my light and wanting to grasp it and keep it for themselves. I continued to do the expo events whenever possible and I kept on doing my work, helping wherever I could. I was happy doing what I did, but still the sense of fulfillment kept nagging at me deep inside.

I religiously kept up my diary, writing down insights about myself, and noting down the symbols that kept popping up in my dreams. Symbols (e.g. eagles, spiders, snakes, cars, trucks, water) could help me learn to understand the language of my soul. I wrote down questions—dozens of questions, all relevant to life; I found that as long as I asked the right questions just before dropping off to sleep, my dreams were guaranteed to bring the insight needed. It was as though I was forming a bridge between the subconscious and the consciousness of my soul. I began to be more structured in my efforts to consciously develop my intuitive skills and abilities. This was all in a vain attempt to become a bigger and better person to align to what I had now decided to call my own true north.

I understood it would take constant application to develop my senses, so every day I practised. I sat in meditation three times a day for ten minutes. I would allow the silence to clear my mind and wipe the thoughts away until I became enshrouded in that warm blanket feeling, as though I was ultimately connected to all things. Deep inside me I knew, that if I could develop my senses to the point of extreme clarity; then my senses could guide me, warn me, and keep me out of trouble. I have to laugh when I think how naive I was back then. I truly believed that if I were a good, honest, and kind human being, facing life with courage; then things would be easier. I still had so much to learn, and the inner questions just kept coming. I had no idea where my journey was leading me, but I was following along with every ounce of my body, mind, and spirit.

The only thing I was sure about was that I was determined to somehow fix the troubles and the sadness that had so doggedly followed my every move. I have no doubt that the ultimate means by which humanity will achieve its awakening is through people being called to be aware of their experiences, as I have been. Awakening isn't necessarily about the quest for perfection, or the saving of humanity. The journey of every one of us is simply the soul trying to fulfill its need to understand and to ultimately find peace. Life is the call to evolve and to develop our understanding. It is the call to understand the truth—that everything we experience is the result of the choices we make. And, it is the call to understand the subtle subconscious needs and desires which influence our choices. If we are lucky, age brings us closer and closer to being honest with ourselves. With self-honesty, comes an unshakable trust in the truth behind our intention, and also trust in the alignment of that intention with our higher 'best' selves. This leads us to live life in a much more peaceful manner, if we are lucky! It would seem however, that there are some people who are not destined to become aware, and some are certainly not ready to come to peace within their own skins.

Not every person is the same, thank God. It would be a very boring life if we all were the same, that is. Awareness is not for everyone. Many people are not compelled by the drive to become better tomorrow than they are today. For the most part, these people believe they are alone in the world and that 'when you die, you're dead', it's that simple. The irony of it all is that often a person who seeks self-awareness, ends up married to someone who is not interested in anything to do with spiritual development. We are like angels who have found physical anchors on earth; we seek awareness, and yet tie ourselves to a very mortally bound soul, in order that we do not lose hold on reality. If we did not have these anchors, we would, surely as the sun rises each day, find our minds shattering and our lives becoming as dysfunctional as the reality depicted in *Alice in Wonderland*.

My wise friend Charlemagne once said to me, 'The greatest gift in life is to learn to live it,' simply that. So, enjoy every moment as if it is your last. Spend time with people you love, and show them you love them. Walk in the sunshine and see the color of life which surrounds you. Live life, for heaven's sake! Embrace all its banquet has to offer. Charlemagne taught me that when we live in truth, we then live in freedom. It is from this freedom that we build solid lives that lead others by example. Until we become aware we have a choice as to how we respond, many of our decisions in life are made for the wrong reasons. We make them to please others, or because we think it's what we have to do. Often we don't know we have a choice; we simply do the best we can with the limited understanding we have. Then when we look honestly at our lives, we are shocked because we realize we have not listened; we have not honored the self. We often compromise our truth (our principles/values) in order to have what we thought we wanted, or to feel safe, or to reach our goals.

I thought my job would be something I could do easily, and it was. The problem was, I didn't always agree with how the corporation wanted me to do things, and I didn't like the fact that they wasted so much money—it left my head spinning. My job was to identify eighteen people who hadn't worked in over two years and then to mentor them and teach them life skills which would get them back into the workforce. I didn't find it hard at all. Most of what I did was common sense. Many of the people I found had learning disabilities, which put them ill at ease with taking on responsibilities in some areas. I could easily understand how they might feel embarrassed, afraid of rejection, or of being judged; so I set out to change the system. In the finish, the most important thing I accomplished in that role was not about the results; it was about the fact that I took those eighteen plus people and made sure they walked away with a higher self-worth than when they met me. Some of those people went on to become kindergarten teachers, business owners, trades-people; and one, an actor.

At the same time as I was working at this job, I was busy with my own work on weekends—going to expos, doing my spiritual readings, and counseling. Most importantly perhaps, I was beginning to learn how to read and write so I could write the book which was bubbling up in the back of my mind. Even as an adult, my learning disability meant that I had great difficulty comprehending the written word. I had never been able to spell because I reversed the letters and I also reversed the numbers in Math. My learning problems had always held me back. It is little wonder that as a child I was embarrassed and shy. To be honest, I didn't know why I couldn't read and write like other people. My one saving grace was that I had persisted in learning to touch-type at high school. So now, I could close my eyes and use the keyboard to try to say what I wanted to say. It was so damn painful! The words didn't flow, the spelling was terrible, and the grammar … well, to me it was just impossible. I have no idea what happened during all those years in English class. Surely, the teachers must have seen I just didn't get it. Maybe they didn't care. Who knows, but all I knew was that the only way I would overcome this was to keep trying. I spent hours writing, hours crying, and hours suffering from headaches, but my determination pushed me onwards. Slowly but surely, the keyboard became my friend, and even though the words I typed on paper were far from perfect, I felt as though I had climbed Mount Everest. I needed to keep stretching; it was as though some invisible force pushed me to learn, to keep trying, and to overcome my limitations—so that one day I would be able to step into synergy with my destiny. I just had to keep going, no matter what!

There is a synergy that surrounds all people and all things in this world. The blessings come when you relax and bring your energy in step with that synergy. We are driven by our need to control, and by our irrational fears and thought processes. These constantly dis-empower us, tricking us into thinking that by working harder, and feeling less, we can escape the suffering caused by our own minds. In the 1980s, I began teaching people to question what they thought. Specifically, this meant questioning why their minds told them they were stupid, or dumb, or no one loved them. I taught people to challenge those beliefs and to look at the reality of their situation. Of course, someone has loved you at some time, so the belief that 'no one loves me' is a lie, a lie we keep telling ourselves over and over again. This is the life of the un-awakened soul. Imagine how you would feel if you didn't have those disempowering thoughts, judgments, criticisms, and self-abusive head games. The world would be so amazing if we, as individuals, could all let go of the biggest war of all, the war going on inside our own heads.

I had now reached the time of my own letting go. Every step was painful. Every step had more questions. My truth and my self-honesty were ever-shifting sands. What was true one day was not true the next, as I dug deeper and deeper into my own subconscious. Pandora's Box had been opened, and before too long, the only thing I would have left would be hope. Illness seemed to be the tool God used to stop me in my tracks. When you can't get out of bed, when your body hurts more than you could ever imagine possible, it does tend to challenge everything you believe.

There are people out there who will tell you that if you are ill, then your illness is generated from a spiritual misalignment. In other words, something is wrong with your thinking and your attitude. This is not always true. At times, yes, I think it is correct. But to disempowered people in this way, does not bring true answers, not in my book anyway. Yes, we do cause ourselves sickness and injury by the thoughts we empower and believe. We may become addicted to our thoughts, to the point where they are what is pushing us to behave in certain ways. This, in turn, often generates more stress than the body can handle. There are however, many other factors involved in health and well-being that may cause illness: genetics, DNA, natural disasters, environmental pollutants, our personal history, and so many pieces of the puzzle. I know it's easy to enter into the game of finding the solution, finding someone to blame for your situation, finding something that needs to be fixed, or labeling something. But, according to our circumstances, we all have choices about where we live, what we eat, and how we behave.

There are some who are not so fortunate as to have the choices that most of us in the developed world enjoy. For example, how can anyone say that a tiny one year old child in Africa has a choice when it comes to poverty, starvation, or abuse? But, to say that it is karma for a child to be born under such circumstances is to me, totally disrespectful to the child and its parents. No, this is not karma. Those of us who are stronger and can, should assist this child to have the level of comfort and wellbeing needed to support its life experience. The only sense I can make of the chaos in this world, is that if everyone were to give a portion of the excess they have (whether it's a penny or a million dollars) to those who have nothing;

then, and only then, would the world be able to rid itself of many of the illnesses which plague the less fortunate. When we give our love, compassion, and understanding, suffering can be lessened. It is the cumulative experience of many individuals awakening to a higher consciousness that potentially can fulfill the destiny of humanity on this earth.

In life, there is one truth I can guarantee. It is, that no matter what you do, where you live, where you go, or where you work, you take yourself with you. The plain and simple fact is, that often fate, destiny, or the universe has to stop us in our tracks every now and then. This is done in order for us to re-evaluate our direction and make critical choices, which in turn affect our lives. The most powerful tool for change is pain and suffering. Nothing propels a person faster or further. I had reached a point where I now had to face the realization that most of my life had been a lie. I had been in situations where I didn't want to be, but I had stayed because I didn't think I had a choice. The end result of that lack of constructive willfulness was that my body became so stressed that my immune system broke down. As a result, I contracted glandular fever and something in Australia we call cat scratch fever (picked up from the scratch of a wild kitten). All this was in addition to another mysterious illness which no one could identify. My health was now in an extremely compromised state.

My life had fallen apart so many times over the years that I had lost count. There were times when I thought I was dying, and times when I thought I was on the verge of madness. There were times when my heart hurt so much I felt it would surely shatter into a million pieces. And yet, today I know that the only time something breaks in life is when it wasn't real anyway. Awakening can be a terribly painful thing. Our very nature pushes us to strive to break the illusions which cause our pain in the first place. How we view our lives—every experience, every rejection, and every loss—brings us one step closer to the God that restores our souls to be greater than we ever imagined they could be.

I had only a couple of thousand dollars in the bank, which would not last long, so I needed to swallow my pride and go on the government sickness benefit. I was alone, and I sensed that fate was going to give me just enough time to reconsider my life's direction and the choices I needed to make, and to let go of whatever needed letting go of. Meanwhile, I still had on my Alice in Wonderland rose-colored glasses, and my magical Dorothy red shoes (Wizard of Oz); I still had no idea of how to let go, surrender to the higher vision, and get out of this predicament. Life had taught me to be personally responsible for my situation and as hard as it would be, I knew I had to take care of myself. I also knew that in my present circumstances, it would be a struggle to find out what it was that God wanted me to do; but I was determined to find out before my chance had passed.

I struggled. God watched on, waiting for me to get tired and surrender to the magic which waited just beyond my line of sight. So often we think we have to be in charge and in control, when in fact all of our thoughts and struggle actually block us from achieving a higher goal. Surrendering is not about giving up, it is in fact learning to move in synergy with the universal tide of consciousness, and following the path of least resistance. Just as God opens the flowers every single day without forcing a single bud, we must learn to open to opportunities only when the time is right. If only we can stop trying to force our lives to be how we think they should be, things will work out.

T.B. Human

I was naive enough to think that I had reached the spiritual place of freedom and I egotistically thought the worst of my struggling was over. Now I would set my course at working out how to do what I wanted to do in life. If I had only known what lay ahead of me, would I have walked this path? I wondered. I am not sure I would have had the courage; however, now that it is all behind me, I wouldn't have missed it for anything. This was a period in my life when I fell in love, and then out of love just as quickly. Men wanted to own and control me; and to be honest, that just didn't sit well with me, at all. So I'd love them and leave them. No one fitted in with the way my life was headed. No one seemed to be able to accept the eccentric creative spiritual me. So I just played. I answered to no one but myself, and actually loved my own company. I found there were times when I was lonely, wishing for that Mr. Right to come along and sweep me off my feet. But in truth, he never would have been able to keep up with the changes in me during those years. I soon began to realize that in order for me to find the love of my life; I first had to become me. I had to turn on the illumined light within my soul, by releasing the patterns of behavior which no longer worked in my life.

I have always had a lot of creative energy; for most of my life it has flowed through me like a power cable. But if that creative energy has no expressive outlet, the frustration and personal discomfort becomes intolerable. Early in life, I had to learn how to focus my big energy and my creative skills. And no matter how sick I was, that mindset was just not going to stop, change, or disappear. I was still living in a unit high on the headland overlooking Duranbar Beach at Tweed Heads. My view of the beaches and sea was magnificent; the blue vista extended as far as the eye could see, uncluttered by any sign of human activity. Tweed Heads is at the southern end of the beautiful Gold Coast strip in Eastern Australia. Life had led me here; my gut feelings and my dreams had shown me the way. I knew my life was about to change again. In this life I had already gone from a country girl, to an island girl…wife, mother, nurse, farmer, miner, therapist, teacher, co-coordinator, workplace trainer; and finally, writer. Every time I grew comfortable with what I was doing in my life, it seemed that something would happen to wipe it all away. And so, it didn't come as a complete surprise when the program I had been running came to an early closure. The government pulled the funding, despite the fact that my incubator was actually very successful. My health was fragile, and so once again all I could do was to trust that my welfare and my survival would be provided for.

Life at that time was so very different from the life I led back in 1968, or even in 1994 when I moved to this place in the sun. When I think about it, it's even further removed than I ever could have imagined from the day in the operating room in 1976. That was the day when my life force left me and my world was rocked to the core. That was the day I stepped through the veil of life and death. In that moment of death, my view of life in this world changed forever. With that experience, my consciousness completely altered. I have come to the conclusion that consciousness is different things to different people, dependent upon what stage of evolution a person is embracing. Today, I am a very different person from the person who began this journey. I guess that is what I came into this life to do— my task has been to grow and become conscious of all things about myself. It takes a whole lot of strength to overcome those limitations we are born into; you can't bake a cake without cracking a few eggs. Ultimately, aspects of you and your life will shatter as you move forward in your journey. It's simply the way of nature. Any part of your life that no longer serves you will fall away to make space for the new. The faster you change and evolve, the faster changes spin your way; and ultimately, what you think is truth today will no longer apply tomorrow.

There are no easy fixes in life. Becoming self-aware won't happen overnight, but it will happen. Our lives are the direct result of how we think, how we process information, and the choices we make in response to circumstances. We can make informed choices, or we can simply run on autopilot and react to every little thing; it's up to us. I would like to think that my role in writing this manuscript has been to help you be aware that you have choices, to show you that there are other ways of looking at life experiences, and to reassure you that we often see only a tiny part of the picture. For most of our lives, our actions are prompted by subconscious assumptions and presumptions; all of which are fed by our insecurities, fears, beliefs, and values. Every moment of every day, we make the best choices we can, based upon the information and skills at our disposal. We cannot do what we do not know how to do, and one of the biggest problems we have as human beings is that we don't know what we don't know. We just do the best we can with what we have. We blunder along with all our past conflicts, confusions, and joys coloring our reality as we go. We often focus so intently on the problems that we make them bigger, blowing them out of all proportion. What we should be doing is looking at where we want to go, and letting the path open up according to our belief and guided by our intuition.

When I speak about being aware that there are other ways to look at life's experiences, and that we need to see the bigger picture, sometimes that can hit very close to home. In my own case, after years of my family telling me to go out and get a real job, I came to the sad conclusion that they had no idea who I was, or what I was capable of. What they saw was what made them feel safe—the mother, the wife, the lover, and the sister who needed protection from herself. I questioned how it was that they didn't see more. I questioned that a perfect stranger could often see more of my spiritual side and relate better to my purpose than those I loved could. I wondered sometimes if it was because there had been so much conflict over the course of my life, where those I loved most, had been affected by the choices I had made. I thought if they could see the truth, would they still judge me? Does anyone have the right to judge another person? After all aren't we here to learn from our experiences?

Years ago, I gave up trying to get my family to see the big picture of what I have been working on for the last thirty years. I feel I am like one of the magnificent magicians. I do what I do … but people are so absorbed in their own stuff that they very rarely see what I am actually doing. A magician often misdirects the audience's attention so he can complete the trick. You never know how it was accomplished. You are focusing so intently on trying to see what is happening, that you don't see what is really happening at all. People just don't have the eyes to see the big picture. This is very true in real life!

My body still screamed at me with pain and fevers from the illness I had contracted. It hurt as if I had been run over by a truck and the aches and pains never seemed to stop. Glandular fever makes you feel extremely tired so for some time, I slept up to eighteen hours a day—a bit like a silkworm entering its cocoon and waiting to be reborn as a beautiful butterfly. The long periods of sleep made out-of-body adventures a common occurrence. Ever since my near-death experience many years before, I had no problem accepting the fact that the soul could separate from the body and travel, while still being alive and connected to the body. I didn't know what made it happen, only that it did at regular intervals. I kept feeling like I was being sucked out of my body, almost as if someone somewhere was calling me. As my illness progressed, the need for sleep grew, and the longing to be with someone I had never met consumed me with a passion.

Sleep was so welcome because, when asleep, I was with the man of my dreams, the love I secretly yearned to find. There were also times when I seemed to travel to other lives, even to other realms, and other civilizations. I don't know if these were real or my imagination was just making them up in order to satisfy my psyche's need to have a reason for everything. Being unwell meant there was more time for sleep. My body hurt so much with the pain of the swelling in my joints that sleep brought relief. There were so many out-of-body adventures and so many experiences, they could fill a book on their own. There was one particular experience where I remember a sense of being called to account for my life. It was as though I was being called to appear before the board of a big company to account for my choices and actions. In my dream, I was called before a panel of eight people. There they sat in front of me, all wearing robes, all looking like something out of a sci-fi movie. Holly crap! I thought it was my day of judgment! Apparently I had chosen to do something in this lifetime. I had chosen to come into this life to achieve the goal of helping humanity evolve. My challenge was to create something that would use all my knowledge, not just from this lifetime, but from previous lifetimes. I was to create something that would enable people to stop fighting and to understand each other. It sounds bizarre when I write this; that's for sure. I was to be the messenger—a tool of hope and peace apparently—and all I could think was, Why me God? I woke from the experience, not knowing if it was the fever from being ill or whether I had really had some other-worldly experience. I just couldn't shake the feeling of it having been an alternate valid reality. It was almost haunting in the fact that it kept creeping into my mind at every opportunity. I could rationalize this and say it was just the fever working its magic, but the feelings were so haunting, as if what had happened connected deep in my soul, making it squirm.

I loved living there in my apartment; the view was an extension of my inner peace. High on a hill, away from the mad rush and bustle, its total calm was uninterrupted by people or the busyness of city life. Life was very simple and very easy as I had no one to answer to but me. I was single, footloose and fancy-free; and feeling, in spite of the being unwell, that love was just around the corner. I found myself studying brain function and altered states of consciousness. I began researching healing, healing modalities, effects of hypnotism, meditation, and more. I had such a hunger to understand how the human brain worked and how it grew in consciousness. It was like being on a train that was flying down the track at 100 km per hour and being unable to get off. I devoured books by authors including Michael Hutchinson, Deepak Chopra, Shirley MacLaine, Robert Suzuki, and others. I was on a seeker's path, and in a weird and wonderful way, everything made sense. I slept, I read, and I slept some more. Each time I slept, my subconscious would put together the next steps, bringing them into consciousness through lucid dreaming.

Dreams were vivid and many times recurring. I would see discs of images, words, and complex patterns all manifesting as though my vision was of what I would create. There were dreams in which I would see myself playing the children's board game of snakes and ladders. This was all so odd when you think about it. But then, one morning very early at sunrise, I woke with the words, 'Life is just a game.' going 'round and 'round in my head. This was interesting because I do tend to take life too seriously and come to think of it, I had to be one of the most serious people I had ever met. Still suffering the pain of the debilitating glandular fever, I in general felt as though I was suspended and hung in mid-air, just waiting for something, anything, to materialize. My attitude to life was once again leading me forward. Fate had provided me with an opening to reach a little higher, to push a little harder, and to use another aspect of my being to develop another part of me. Everything was for a reason, and all of my life experiences would go into developing this tool for positive change. It was not easy, focusing all that energy into creating something new. My frustration mounted due to the fact I could not go out and live a normal life because I was unwell. Up until recently life had been far more challenging in a positive way. But now I felt I was being blown apart as I struggled to download my knowledge into something tangible.

I was lonely, it was that simple. The man of my dreams was still only in my dreams; and the ones in the physical, well, they just didn't live up to what I wanted in a life partner and lover. A couple of weeks had gone by since the strange dream in which I stood before the panel of elders. I had been doing a lot of sketching, trying to figure out how to make life a game. I had an idea of how I could make a life map, and then use the same process when working with clients to shift their thinking. I had a gut feeling I could break my method down into a set of parts and then apply it, but it was all so vague and far away.

One Sunday morning, I was showing some of my latest

drawings to a friend when he said, 'Do you know what you've got there?'

I looked at him blankly and said, 'Not really. I know it's a drawing, and it symbolizes everything about what enlightenment is to me. What do you mean?'

He was very excited and said, 'You've got the key right there. Don't you see? It's a game. All you need to do now is to develop it.' In an instant, I was able to see the picture from another point of view. Instantly, what had been so elusive became apparent. My awareness changed in that moment and goosebumps ran over me from head to foot. From that moment on, my excitement began to build and enthusiasm immediately replaced the state of frustration in which I had been living. Enlightenment had arrived, and I was one step closer to being able to identify the process of how I would develop my game.

One Sunday evening in 1994, a group of friends sat around my kitchen table, debating the name of this new evolutionary product I had created. Mick, my son-in-law at the time, was the one who had the flash of genius. 'The game is a truism. It is about truth and integrity,' he said. And so the 'Game of Life' was born. From that point on, it was a matter of allowing the ideas to flow unrestricted until they formed the foundations for the game I called *TRUITY - the Game of Life*. In that moment, my life changed forever. This game was about to teach me everything I would need to know to become enlightened. By this, I mean I started to understand how all the pieces of the puzzle would fit together. And once completed, my game would finally reveal to me what it was I was born to do, or so I thought. Developing the board for the game was easy. I dreamt every part of it, and bringing the visions from my dream state to the physical was just a matter of attention to detail. I had been studying brain function and human behavior. My research had disclosed some awesome insights into how human consciousness evolved, so I knew this was going to be some special game—a game that would support people to think in synergy with the soul. I still didn't know exactly how the game design in my head would transpose into a physical product, but I knew I could do it. I knew I was meant to find a way. For days, once again I wrote down all the insights and followed my gut feelings, not entirely sure what it was that I was creating.

I stretched my knowledge of brain function to the maximum. I found myself digging through boxes of notes I had made over the previous five years relating to physiology, stimulus and response, brain chemistry, attitudes, beliefs, and personality traits. I scanned through my library of New Age books to see if there was another elusive ingredient which I could add to the puzzle. I understood that I was creating a game which would teach people how to do what I had innately been able to do, but I was unaware of exactly what I was doing until I asked myself the right question. It had taken me all my life until that moment to learn the process hidden behind all growth in human consciousness. How could I formulate the game questions and then develop a process which would trigger their application for other people? My brain felt as though it would explode with the stretching and the mental gymnastics. I decided to draw a mind map that would help me discover what I knew that I didn't know I knew. And so off I went on another tangent of discovery.

Weeks later, the biggest mind map I have ever seen was lying before me. The drawing was, in itself, a masterpiece of artwork. But still the insight of how I was going to create the tool to help others grow and change eluded me. Insight came little by little over the next weeks, like discrete sparks of electricity accompanied by a feeling of,

'That's it!' which led me on a journey of unbelievable challenge and growth. But for the present time, there was still something that hadn't quite crystallized, something I was not seeing. There was one last piece of information still out of reach. I kept thinking, I know it is so obvious, but what is it I am trying to capture? What is it I am trying to identify so everyone else will benefit from it? What on earth is it? I paced the floor and meditated, and paced the floor again. I used as much of my awareness and resources as could be mustered, and then I gave up. It was then that it all happened.

CHAPTER SEVEN

'*F*ools who should know better.'

Life was good. For a change, it seemed everything was going according to God's plan.

I lived in a magical place where days were golden and the sands of the beach so crystal clean and white. Sometimes I would sit on the shore and watch the whales as they migrated north for the birthing of their calves. My apartment was near the top of a high-rise, located on the headland at the mouth of the Tweed River. I suppose I would have had the best view on the coast, with its unobstructed view of the sea; and high up on the hill, it was as though I could leave the energy of the world's chaos behind me. I was secluded in my tower just like the Lady of Shalott, but I cherished this time of being alone so I could write and not be disturbed. In my tower, the sea inspired my passion for words and my out of body experiences brought me an excitement which enabled my words to manifest. Life at Duranbah Beach was amazing!

When I wasn't writing or sitting on the beach, I was sleeping a lot but it was as though my illness gave me permission to rest. And in that resting I was able to enter another world, a different vibration of frequency. It was a world which this time was filled with the teachings of the Masters. Once again, my dreams were to be the doorway to releasing my Karma, but little did I realize just how intense this journey would become.

Each night, sleep would pull me into a world far separated from my own life. I had become the unwilling spectator in a real-life drama. In my dreams, there was often a man who resembled someone straight out of a James Bond movie. He was tall and handsome with a receding hairline and obviously English, although he wore an Australian army uniform. As this mercenary dressed in black was lowered from a hovering helicopter, I had the strangest feeling that I was him, hanging from a rope over a blackened landscape. I silently looked on as explosives were set and this man in black fought in hand-to-hand combat for his life. The story is almost impossible to tell in one short chapter. I saw things I should never have been privy to.

Each night I would hurry off to bed, excited to see what tonight's dream would bring with Mr. Charming, as I nicknamed him. He was dashing, that's for sure. He seemed to have an air of confidence and importance about him that was appealing and far outweighed any feelings of fear that surrounded the events I was actually tapping into. Who was this man? Why was he in my dreams? What connection could there be between him and me that brought such intense knowing? I was about to find out.

That particular night, and in my dream you understand, I was woken by the sound of a slapping helicopter blade outside my window—whamp! Whamp! whamp! I sat straight up in my bed. There in front of me, hovering outside my window, was a Blackhawk

Helicopter. I sat motionless, unable to move as the man I had been seeing for weeks smiled back at me. In acknowledgement that he recognized me, he gave a quick wave of his hand; then the helicopter turned and flew away. Needless to say, if that wasn't weird enough, what followed is surely the most bizarre story of my life.

The next morning, I had been invited to have lunch with an old friend of mine. Philomena was Irish and a clairvoyant. We were to meet at 11.30 am at the little cafe in the main street of Tweed for some pasta and a glass of wine. I arrived to find Philomena sitting inside the restaurant waiting for me. Her first words were 'Lesley, unfortunately I don't have much time, I have an appointment this afternoon. A friend is helping me to organize some of my new business things.' I took a deep breath. That was all right, I thought to myself. I was planning on seeing a movie anyway. A movie was my usual Sunday afternoon treat. I could sit back and be totally absorbed in someone else's story for a couple of hours. Philomena was someone who understood what my life was like. We shared a common bond in that she too was extremely gifted with psychic ability. Philomena had chosen as her life path to train as a neuro-linguistic program (NLP) practitioner. That, combined with her psychic ability, made her a force to be reckoned with. We ordered lunch and sat chatting about life in general. As she shared with me news about her daughter, I struggled to listen attentively for, if the truth were known, the bizarre experience of my dream the night before was pulling at my mind and heart strings.

Philomena was single, another thing we had in common. 'Have any new interesting men come into your life, Lesley?' she smiled, pushing her long blond hair back from her face. I loved the sound of her voice. Her strong Irish brogue gave me goosebumps.

'No,' I laughed at the thought, 'but I did have an interesting dream about that army major; you know, the Englishman who keeps turning up in my dreams, the one with the ever so posh voice.' With that, I began to giggle like a school girl. I felt silly and excited at the same time, and I believe I actually blushed.

'Come on, tell me more,' Philomena urged. And so, I told her the story of the man who had been coming to me in dreams every night for the last few weeks. I told her what I knew about this man, what his first name was, and that he was a doctor of some sort; I thought that he perhaps held a Ph.D. degree. I told her all the information I had scratched together and specifically that he was a major in the army. With that, Philomena nearly choked on her pasta. Her mouth fell open with the shock, 'My God, Lesley! Do you know where I'm going after we have lunch? I'm going to see … You have just described my friend! He's in the military, he works for military intelligence!' My head was spinning and my heart was racing. I was so excited, I felt as though I was going to explode into a million stars. As you can imagine, I can't write the man's name. So for the purposes of this book, I will call him Mr. Charming, for no other name would suit him. For me though, he turned out to be about as charming as a king cobra.

Philomena and I finished lunch and I gave her my business card. It was one of those cards that had a photo of me in the corner. 'Ok, Lesley, I'm going to give him your card and see what happens. He is psychic too so, if he is aware of you, then I have no doubt he will have something to say.' Philomena waved the card above her head as she walked out of the cafe towards her car. Time would tell, I supposed. The afternoon air was so clear and fresh that I could smell the sea breeze as I crossed the road and headed towards the movie theatre for my welcome afternoon distraction.

After the movie, I headed up the hill to the seclusion and safety of my apartment. It was about 5.30 pm when my phone rang. On the other end was a very excited Philomena, 'Lesley, you're not going to believe this!' The words were flying out of her mouth so fast you could hardly make sense of the Irish accent. 'I told him I had a friend I thought he should meet and handed him your card. The next thing, he turns to me and says, 'Why are you handing me a photo of my next wife? I don't even think he realized what he said. (She was giggling so much, she gasped.) He looked so shocked. He said he's going to call you.' Philomena was beside herself. 'This is him, Lesley. I am sure this is the man of your dreams!'

Well, man of my dreams or not, it all felt so surreal, as if it was too good to be true. So I waited ... one day, two days; then, early in the afternoon of the third day, my phone rang. 'Hello, my name is ... Is that Lesley?' I went weak at the knees. It was that same voice that sophisticated polished British accent, like someone who had attended a private school in London. We talked, but not for long. He had actually called to ask me to visit him the following Sunday. My heart was flipping out in every direction as somehow I managed to mumble 'Yes.' and get the directions. Sunday came too soon. I was still so nervous and so dumbfounded that my psychic dreams had actually brought me face-to-face with this modern-day James Bond.

I anxiously walked up the concrete driveway towards the two storey brick and tile home. It was nothing flash; actually, a little scruffy for someone who was supposed to be so important. I rang the doorbell and waited. I remember thinking I had no idea what I was going to say. How could I tell him that I had seen what I had seen of his life, and how could I explain how I knew what I knew? It was bewildering to say the least. My life was about to change forever but not in the way I thought it was going to change. 'Nice to meet you, Lesley,' he said, as he reached out and took my hand. 'You're shaking. Are you nervous? Why are you nervous?' His voice cut through the afternoon silence like a hot knife through butter. Only slightly reassured, I walked inside and was immediately ushered into a strange sort of room under the house. Computers lined the walls and stuff was everywhere, there were flight simulators and all sorts of gadgets. I had no idea what most of it was, but it looked to be serious stuff. 'Please take a seat and make yourself comfortable. Would you like coffee or tea?' he enquired. Thinking back now, I can't remember what I said or even if I said much at all. It was so bizarre. Standing in front of me was a man I had never met before that I knew more about than I probably should. We chatted for a while and feeling more comfortable by now, I decided that I would just answer his questions honestly. I would tell him that it was my friends 'in spirit' who had told me about his life. Then he asked me what I knew and of course, being the trusting naive woman I can be at times, I just blurted out all the different stories. Mr. Charming looked quite taken aback and with sternness in his voice queried, 'Lesley, I need to know who told you all that information.' I had a very quaint habit of calling my spirit companions 'the fellows' in the same way you would refer to an old friend. I often commented on spirit communication by saying, 'The fellows told me this.' or 'the fellows told me that.' Mr. Charming's mannerisms by now were becoming a little overbearing. He leaned his six foot five frame slightly over me sitting in my chair and pushed the point, 'This is serious Lesley. Who are the fellows?'

I giggled, becoming nervous; I always giggled when I was nervous. 'You know, the fellows upstairs,' I shrugged, 'my helpers. I don't know why, but they showed me what you do. And they told me who you are and that we were meant to meet. Why?'

The soft-touch interrogation continued. There were more and more questions and Mr. Charming became more and more demanding that I disclose my source, 'Was it the CIA? ... the KGB ... MI5?' I just kept on laughing; this was so funny. How on earth would he even think someone like me would have anything to do with anything like that! I had no idea what I had stumbled headlong into. I had no idea of the danger I was in, or how it would nearly break my mind and destroy my life. He was so attractive—like a panther—strong and muscular, yet agile. The man just oozed sexuality in a way I had never experienced before. I felt like a helpless schoolgirl, hypnotized in an instant by his authoritative voice and his deep blue eyes. The thought running through my mind was, Haven't we met somewhere before? I felt bizarrely all knowing of this man, and attracted to him, and that was such a dangerous mix. He was like me, I knew it; yet, he was not like me. His energy was different; more like the opposite of mine. Mr. Charming must have noticed my confusion and thought he might do better if he changed his tact. He adopted a friendlier approach and began trying to flatter and seduce me to find out his answers.

I had by now been in his home, in the room full of computers and flight simulators where he worked, for over an hour. I was more than a little overwhelmed and so I politely made my move to leave. 'I must be going now,' I stammered, as I rose out of my chair and headed for the door.

He rose apologetically. 'I'm sorry, I didn't mean to interrogate you, but you know things you shouldn't,' he said, placing emphasis on the word 'shouldn't'. Attentively, he walked me to the door by placing his hand on my elbow, like an old fashioned gentleman. He was so close that I felt alive with electricity. Just his touch on my arm was enough to make me burn with desire but at the same time I was very afraid of where things might lead. I had to get out now! 'You do know I will have to make a report about meeting you,' he paused, looking deep into my eyes as he said the words. (I think he was trying to gauge how I would respond.) 'I will make the report; it's not every day that I meet someone with your talents,' he said. He smiled that seductive smile as he put his hooks in a little deeper, 'I go to the Spiritualist Church every Sunday. Would you like to come with me next week?' How could I refuse!

The week passed in a flurry of activity. Work was busy, life was good, and I was walking ten feet off the ground. Sunday arrived all too soon. It was around 6 pm when I picked Mr. Charming up in my car and we headed off to a nearby suburb to a Spiritualist Church meeting. As we drove, he asked lots of questions—about me, about my life, about my children; but mostly, he wanted to hear about the dreams I had experienced of his life. This man was dashing, polite, strong, and truly the man of my dreams. What was a girl to do but fall head over heels in love with him! My eyes were blinded by his charm. My heart took over my head as once again, I rushed in where angels feared to tread. I think Mr. Charming could have told me the sky was made of fairy floss and the stars were jewels, and I would have believed him at that moment. I can't remember if it was our second or third date. We were sitting in the car after church when he turned to me, taking my hand, 'Lesley,' he paused, looking intense; 'will you do me the honor of becoming my wife?' He was shaking and so was I. Without even stopping to get my breath, for the first time in my life, I didn't hesitate and said 'Yes'. We kissed a kiss that felt as though the earth had moved, accompanied by fireworks and lightning. But although I didn't know it, all hell was about to break loose in the name of revenge. My heart raced as he spoke to me in fluent French and my feet went to jelly. I gave my heart and soul to this man, and I gave it willingly. It was a pact with the devil himself and I never suspected a thing. Kiss a girl who is looking for love, ask her to marry you, and she will tell you anything you want to know. This was his intention, I have no doubt. But guess what? It didn't work. Why? Simply because I had been telling him the truth all along. My intuition always showed me what I needed to know; it was that simple. There was nothing more to it than that.

And so, my nightmare began. The first couple of weeks were the happiest weeks of my life. I floated about on 'cloud nine' and my heart was singing so loudly I could not hear the guidance of my soul. His questions kept coming but like a fool, I trusted this man with every ounce of my body, mind, and soul. Now, you could say at this point, 'Well, wasn't your intuition supposed to protect you from bad experiences? Weren't you guided to keep yourself safe?' And the answer to that is both 'Yes' and 'No'. Intuition works when we listen to it but it's our choice whether we listen to it or not. You see, that is the thing about free will, we can completely stuff up our lives at any moment we choose. That's why it's called free will.

The first sense I had of something not being right was very subtle. I noticed a feeling, as if someone had been in my apartment. It was a presence different to my own that I had not felt before. I don't know how to explain it fully, but as I turned the key in the lock that day, I instantly felt that someone else had been in the room. The hair on the back of my neck stood straight up. It was a tangible sense of another person's energy, someone I didn't know. Then the creepy feeling of being watched began. You know, the car that follows you too long and the person you keep seeing everywhere you go. My phone had clicks and taps on it and there was the constant feeling that someone was listening in. There was an overwhelming feeling of a nasty energy creeping in and intruding in my life.

My man had not yet become my lover, but Mr. Charming was playing this fish like a prizewinning catch would be played. He was gentle and yet persistent in his quest to land the prize. He gave the impression he was letting his guard down slowly. Although note, I said 'impression'. I don't know if it was calculated or it was just the fact he was also falling in love with me. Then one night in August, all hell broke loose. Mr. Charming broke the news to his wife that he was leaving her, and I don't think either of us was prepared for the onslaught that followed—her screaming, manic phone calls began. She even went so far as to make up false 'Wanted!' posters and sent them out to stores and local businesses. She was mentally deranged, that's for sure. She was convinced I was a child killer named Lesley—how absolutely bizarre!

This woman was about to make my life and his life a living hell. She not only started a campaign locally to destroy me, but also went outside of the box. She went to the highest powers within my 'soon to be' lover's military intelligence circle to report us both. One night together is all we ever had, one tiny space where for the first time in my life I felt bizarrely safe. Our love was strong and at that moment in time, there was no other time. The world stopped, just for that one night. As the sun rose and I began to wake, it was the strangest feeling I have ever experienced—I did not know where I ended and where he began. It was as though our two bodies had melded into one and we would remain one for all eternity. We said our goodbyes, neither of us aware of what was about to unfold.

That is the day the reign of terror started. I was being watched and being monitored with a vengeance. There was a warning phone call from Mr. Charming telling me to hold on, and not be overly disturbed by anything that was about to come my way. But I never for one moment thought I would begin to feel so compromised. Within days, I had become so scared that I tried to keep someone with me at all times. I needed an explanation but what I received was silence. Mr. Charming had gone to ground. There was no phone contact and there were no explanations. Like a ghost, he had gone. It was weeks before I would see him again; but finally, one day there was a phone call in which he said that he wanted to come and explain. Apparently, my talking about him had blown his security cover and he had been called to be accountable. Later, I was told he had been taken away for interrogation and an accountability grilling. It seems he had broken protocol by having an affair with me. This was indeed considered a serious breach of protocol.

Little by little, tiny pieces of the story came out, but they were only ever fragments. During previous years of service, he had been involved in what are called 'black operations'. Because of my psychic ability, I had actually exposed him for who he was, for what he was, and for what he had done. He told me stories during our time together—stories I still am not willing to repeat. I should add that he would only reveal his stories when I told him what I saw (what I already knew) of his life in my dreams or visions.

The most bizarre thing of all was that, apparently at the time of our meeting, his job was to seek out and test psychics to be trained by the military for undercover information gathering. In the end, I found out that the reason he turned up on my radar was in fact because he had been investigating me and my skills, nothing more. In the weeks that followed, his life was almost destroyed by my awareness. My life, on the other hand, became a hunted, haunted hell, and the focus of people you just don't want to upset. All I wanted was to be left alone. My heart was breaking into a million pieces and I cried more than I could ever imagine, asking once again, 'Why me God, why me?'

CHAPTER EIGHT

Allana's Story
'Thank you, my dearest friend.'

After the devastation of the finish of my relationship with Mr. Charming, I threw myself into work. I had a mission, and by hell I was going to fulfill it. Keeping busy was my way of not thinking too much about my own problems, and by turning my attention to helping other people, I found that it made my problems seem insignificant. Life went on. It was 1994; I still lived at Duranbah and worked at the Business Enterprise Centre. I had also been learning a great deal about patents, trademarks and branding to bring my board game to a point where it was almost through the initial stages of development. I knew that it had the potential to help millions of people deal with everyday life problems and so, I was eager to eventually market it. Occasionally, I would invite a group of friends over to play the game so that we could try it out and test it in many ways. I was lucky enough to have doctors, psychologists, social workers, nurses, and more within my network. But I needed cash ... so I would go and do healing work at the expos, and readings for those who requested them. On this particular day, I was a feature exhibitor at the Brisbane Expo. By 9.30 am my bookings for the day were already full; this was normal as my expo days were always booked out. And so, I began my day with my preparatory exercises of self-balancing, clearing, and grounding of the space. For the next fourteen hours my energy, my life and my problems would disappear as I became a clear channel for whatever my clients needed. It was about lunchtime when I stopped for a cup of tea (I never ate much during a day of booked sessions because eating diverted my energy, causing me to get tired very quickly.). As I walked out to the hallway, I had a strange feeling, as though someone's eyes were burning a hole in my back. I turned around to see a Maori woman staring straight at me. As soon as she knew she had my attention, she walked up and offered her hand. 'Hi, my name is Liz; I have a friend who needs your help. You are the one I was told to find. Please, can you come and meet her?' She had an air about her of knowing what she wanted. Her energy was clear and strong, this was a powerful Maori lady with energy to be respected; I didn't ask questions. She wrote an address and a name on a piece of paper and handed it to me. Then, in a flash, she was gone.

Two days later, I stood in the street of a Brisbane suburb, wondering what on earth this was all about. I knew it was not my place to question where my intuition was leading me. If something felt right, you did it. I had been called, and I would help in whatever way I could. I walked up the stairs to the door of a flat and knocked. When the door opened, a thin Maori lady appeared; she had short, cropped hair and looked about my age. The moment I saw her, I felt as though I had known her forever. It was such a strange feeling, as if destiny was taking my hand and opening a door. I was welcomed with open arms; and more than that, by an open heart. A young girl played in the lounge room, while several other people were sitting around in various places as though waiting to check me out; I definitely felt as though I was being inspected. 'Hello, I am Allana,' she said. 'I am so glad to meet you.' With that, she gave me another hug, and while giving me that hug, her belly kicked me. I had no idea that Allana was pregnant. 'Wow!' she said, 'That was his first kick. He likes you, Lesley.' And from that moment on, my life would never be the same.

The story was that Allana had been diagnosed with breast cancer … in the same week she was told she was pregnant. Her decision was not to have treatment because she wanted to give her son (She knew it was a boy right from the start.) the best chance at a long healthy life. Unfortunately, the type of cancer she had was extremely aggressive, and she knew that even if she did have the treatment, there would be no guarantees where her life expectancy was concerned. Within minutes, my bond to Allana was set to endure for eternity. As a matter of fact, I am sure it started long before this lifetime. Allana was my soul sister, the other half of me. From the instant we met, I knew that the bond spirit had formed between us would compel me to be her helper. I loved her more than words can say, and that seems so silly, seeing we hardly knew each other in this life. We both recognized the bond of friendship between us; it was one that could not be measured in time and space. We were 'sisters in Spirit', forever bound by respect and love.

Over the coming months, I observed Allana's inner strength and courage. I shared in her tears, helping her to come to terms with how her journey in this life was to end, and helping her find peace. When she was weak, I became her strength; I gave my energy freely in every way I could. Being a part of her journey was probably the most humbling experience of my life. In that one short year, I learnt so much from Allana. Love truly is putting yourself aside to be there for someone else when they need you.

Time moved on quickly; so much was to happen in my own life between the day I met Allana and the day I would share too, in her joy at the birth of her son. Allana struggled with her fate, exploring every type of alternative therapy, and trying every avenue to stem the fast-paced growth of the cancer in her breast. Each week we would get together for a healing session, in which I would simply send energy to her baby, ensuring he was settled and happy. I was her anchor during that time. But Allana's courage was so amazing; I have never seen courage like that in another human being! And her devotion to her unborn baby son and her family was something to be admired—totally.

The baby was due on 12 April; however, medical intervention in the form of a caesarean section was necessary. And so, on 15 February 1995 with bated breath, we stood in the hospital waiting room awaiting the news that all was well, despite the baby being twelve weeks premature. John Boy was tiny, only two and one-half pounds in weight. His head was no bigger than the size of an orange, and he himself was not much more than the size of a skinned rabbit. But he was safe; our boy was born, a little miracle that would change all of our lives forever! I felt so overwhelmed that day, seeing the mixed emotions of Allana's family—the joy in celebration of new life, and the tears in knowing Allana's time was near. Ominously, immediately after the birth, Allana was whisked away for further surgery to remove her left breast.

After her surgery, Allana looked as though light shone from every pore of her being; she literally glowed with light and love. Her aura was perfect, appearing healed and golden, and extending three feet out from her body. She was an angel in human form. Only once before had I seen light like this; that was four hours before a young girl was killed in a car smash back in Woolgoolga. I cried. I sobbed. I knew 'the light' was coming; it would only be a matter of time. What could I say ... nothing!

The following weeks were a blur. Endless days were spent at the hospital, sitting at Allana's side. We talked about life, we talked about death, and we shared our grief.

John's strength was growing; soon he was taking 5 ml of milk and then 10 ml. He was a fighter, that's for sure. Finally, he was out of the humidicrib, which had helped his lungs develop, and into his mother's arms. As John's strength grew, his mother's weakened. They spent twenty-four hours a day together. She just held him and talked to him, telling him all the things she would never get to say in person when he was old enough to understand. My friend tried everything to stay alive; her determination was immense and admirable—my sadness was overwhelming. We truly were 'sisters in spirit' for having been through this heart-rending experience together. My life would never be the same for having known this amazing lady.

Some of Allana's family didn't like the fact that we were such close friends; they did not welcome my presence. I don't think they understood this bond which had grown between us. Maori people often have strong views on letting outsiders into the inner circle when it comes to health, caring, and family. Others had accepted me, like Allana's sister Bubby and her Aunty Bella. The only thing that mattered to me was keeping my friend comfortable and at peace. I wanted to wrap her up and make her better. I wanted to see her grow old with her children around her. I wanted her to live.

Soon Allana was released from hospital. Days were precious as we all knew every moment counted. But Allana was not a person to have negative thoughts. She went about her day as best she could, and tears were kept hidden behind closed doors. She would fight this; she wanted to live. Her precious children were kept close; Allana comforted her daughter who struggled emotionally, not old enough to understand the enormity of the situation. The house became a hive of activity with people coming and going; Allana spent every moment loving her family and everyone who came close.

I remember so clearly the day she asked me for a commitment I thought I just could not make, or keep. 'Lesley,' she said, 'I want you to do something for me.' (She looked down nervously and reached out to take my hand.) 'Will you look after my children for me? I want you to raise my children.' I was totally overwhelmed. There had been so many shared tears, so much between us. But this…

'Allana, I can't do that,' I answered, squeezing her hand. At that time, I was running a company with twenty staff. There just was not enough of me to go around. I would let the kids down; and besides that, it was not my place. I felt so torn; my heart was breaking and there was nothing I could do! I had learnt in life, never to make a promise I couldn't keep. So when I finally relented and made the promise to always be there for her family, and always watch over them, I knew it was a commitment which would change my life forever.

After Mr. Charming broke my heart and during the time when Allana was sick, my own life was still in chaos. It was a struggle to make ends meet and I was busy trying to develop the idea for the board game. It was all quite stressful. The only way I kept going was to make sure I did my spiritual practices each day—time for meditation, time for writing, and time to work through my own issues.

Finally, the day came when Allana was released from hospital and returned home with John Boy. Endless days were spent lying, just cuddling the child she knew she would not physically see grow into manhood. My role as a friend and healer was simply to listen, to give energy, to help her be comfortable, to love her unconditionally, to cry with her, to hug her, to be her friend far beyond the boundaries of life; and above all, to put her needs above my own pain at seeing her condition deteriorate.

Three months later, while I was working at an expo in Gladstone, I had a vision of a white owl looking at me square in the face; I knew her time was near. A phone call confirmed my feelings. I took an early plane back to Brisbane and went straight to the hospital. My dearest friend was only hours away from death. Hours passed, people came and went, and we waited for the family to arrive from New Zealand. Allana's husband, Murray, quietly comforted his wife–his love–and there was no way to ease the pain of what was about to come. I cried, and I cried. At one point, Allana turned to me and said, 'Lesley, don't cry. You know I have to go. I have to help you from the other side. It's ok.' In her moment of need, here she was trying to comfort me; to give me strength, and to help all of us deal with what she knew was inevitable. On that day, I had no idea of just how relevant Allana's words were. In time to come, she would in fact be the messenger who came back from beyond death, to save my life.

Later that same day, all the family arrived from New Zealand— Bubby, Aunty Bella, Patricia, and Murray's Mum Rita. All the relatives (in body and in Spirit) had arrived, everyone who was closest to Allana. Murray and their daughter Janine were there, as well as other family members—Allana's brothers, their wives and children. I made my silent exit; I knew there was nothing more that I could do. My intuition was Allana would pass at 5.25 pm so I returned to my flat in Tweed Heads and waited. At 5.25 pm I was standing in the kitchen when I felt death pass through me. It's something I cannot describe and do it proper justice. I had felt death before but never so personally. It was as though part of me left and moved on to that other plane. With that flash of energy, I fell to the floor—unconscious. Waking to find myself lying on the cold tiles, I sobbed. I knew my friend had passed, and I knew all I could do was to wait for the phone call. That was 5 September. Allana was just five days older than me; both of us were in our forty-second year. She was far too young to die. It broke my heart to see that there was nothing anyone could do but to mourn her passing, and to watch over the family she had lovingly left behind. Her passing left a whole in my life, and a fresh awareness of just how precious life truly is.

CHAPTER NINE

'Know What Is Right'

My mother's time was coming; her health was failing and at eighty-two years of age, her poor little body had endured about all it could take. Family discussions were held and it was decided that after the collapse of my bizarre relationship with Mr. Charming, I would be the one to move home to help care for my mother. Although my health was fragile from the mysterious virus I had contracted, I was in good spirits. However, doubts and insecurities mounted as the emotional wounds of the last months, along with the stress brought about by my mother's frail health, were almost too much for my sensitivity to bear. My heart was aching from the loss of a very dear friend. Why did things like this happen to good people? Why did God see fit to take a young mother away from her family? There were just so many unanswered questions.

The break-up with Mr. Charming also weighed heavily upon my soul. I still craved his presence, and I was angry; I felt betrayed and confused. How could a man love so passionately and yet behave with so much indifference? Several times over the last weeks my apartment had been searched. By whom and for what reason, I have no real clue. The searches had been carried out with a delicate touch; things were moved slightly, drawers were rearranged. But the most pervasive feeling was one of invasion of my privacy. I had no idea what they expected to find. Maybe they really did think me to be a spy. I doubt if I will ever know. I had found things out, things I never should have known. Some of those things made my hair stand on end with fear. Even the story about where this man came from and the crimes his mother had committed, had to make me question the sanity of the man. My family worried for my physical safety and, to be honest, so did I. I had never been so scared in my life; I never knew if I would, pardon the pun, 'wake up dead.'

So, for my own safety, I went to live with my sister and mother in my brother's house in Brisbane. This was not the ideal everyone wants to achieve, but it worked out well for us all. At least I felt safe there, or I did for a short while. I made the best of the change. Each day I would wake to see the early morning sun flickering through the dark green leaves of the mango tree in the garden. Sitting quietly, I would close my eyes and turn my face to the sun, eager to soak up the feeling of warmth that renewed my body with strength and life. Occasionally, from its hiding place somewhere high in the branches, a tiny bird would sing, carrying its joy of life with every note to every part of my being. Or I would watch a butterfly as it delicately flitted from blossom to blossom and then rested on the leaf of a tree to catch its breath. I smiled as I pondered—that butterfly was me. Somehow, I felt God had provided me with a splash of grace to renew, gain strength, catch my breath, and then fly courageously onwards into the unknown. Not a day passed that I didn't thank God for the glimpse of peace which temporarily filled my life. For a moment in time, everything was perfect.

There were still occasions though, when I felt the heartache of the shattering of love and hoped somehow that my relationship with Mr. Charming would fix itself with time. I wanted to believe this man would be my Prince Charming and carry me off to have a wonderful life. But that was a whim far removed from reality I'm afraid, and I had to be content with Mr. Charming keeping contact discretely from a distance; or should I say, keeping an eye on me. This was a fact my family was not at all happy with. Perhaps I should have paid more attention to their concerns, for it was during a phone conversation one day that he asked the most bizarre question of me. I still don't know why he asked it—He wanted to meet my mother! He claimed … he wanted to ask her if he could marry me; he wanted her approval before she passed away. He revealed to me that as a result of our affair, his high level security clearance had been breached and he had been demoted. He insisted … that he loved me and, if I were patient, everything would be sorted out and we could have a good and happy life together. He kept on reassuring me that as soon as the government got off his back our lives and our plans could proceed; he insisted life would return to normal. So, like a fool in love, I let him come to our home and I cautiously introduced him to my mum. It was a polite conversation. Mum offered him a cup of tea and general pleasantries were exchanged. It didn't take long and Mr. Charming made his excuses and left; I gather he got what he wanted. I don't think that was all as it was made to seem. Who knows why he wanted to meet Mum. Instead of asking her for my hand, he announced his intention to make me his wife and stated that he hoped she was agreeable.

My mother was livid as he headed out the door without so much as a glance back. The moment he was beyond hearing our voices, my mother turned to me and said, 'I want you to promise me something, and I mean it! Don't ever marry that man! You promise me now, you hear me!' I had never seen my mother so angry and serious. 'That man is evil.' Her warm brown eyes had taken on the look of an eagle as she tapped the benchtop laminex with the long fingernail of her index finger …tap…tap…tap! 'You mark my words,' she was shaking with rage, 'That man is evil; he is a spy!' How could she know what he had told me in secret? How did she see this? 'I'm telling you, he is a *spy!*' She took a deep, wheezing breath as she tried to regain control. 'He doesn't work for who you think he does.' The look on my mother's face, I will remember until the day I die. I am still baffled by her response to his presence. Who was my mother? What was her story? I wish I had thought to ask her more, but I suppose I remained too shocked for days. I have never seen my mother like that—not ever!

In the days and weeks that followed, I discovered a whole new side to my mother. It turned out, she was even more psychic than I was. In the months before she passed away, I finally understood the real woman behind the woman I thought I knew. This mild-mannered English woman had another side that none of us had ever seen. She had carried more than one secret for most of her life. She had the gift of sight, the power to see Spirit, and the ability to see things that remained hidden to most people's eyes. During the war she used her gift; in exactly what way though, I'm not sure. No wonder she recognized a spy, maybe she had encountered one herself! All of her life she had kept these things to herself. She had never acknowledged or spoken of these gifts to another living soul … except me. Her secret went with her to the grave. Another piece of the puzzle was falling into place. It was another clue as to why I was the person I had become; and with that clue, I had a feeling of being not so weird, after all.

T.B. Human

On this particular day, I had quite a lot to think about, so I found my favorite place on the back balcony of the house under the mango tree to sit and contemplate the day's events. Off in the distance, I could hear the peak-hour traffic as all manner of people rushed and bustled about on their way to and from work. I wondered how many of them were happy with their lives. With a deep sigh, I wondered at life. And inside of me, I acknowledged that in spite of it all, life did go on. If I gave you an orange and you took one quarter from that orange, it would equal the portion of my life's experience I have written about in this manuscript. The events of my life have been so many, and the experiences so vast, that it is difficult to know what to include in this manuscript and what to leave out. If I wrote about all my experiences, no one would believe me; sometimes I can hardly believe them myself. However, it is my understanding that we often spend far too much time focusing on the negatives of the past, when at any moment we can just let them go and move on. In order to do this however; we must let go, not only of our physical clinging to the hurt and pain, but also of the beliefs and values which interfere with our perception of life. In order to be at peace and clear to make decisions, we must release the past. And, we must also release all worry about the future from our minds, bodies, and souls.

Like it or not, life is often like a black comedy. My sense of humor, even in the most dreadful of times, gives me the ability to laugh at myself and turn hardship into valuable insights. I use those insights to strengthen my resolve to press onwards and to achieve. I am a visual linguist; this means I'm a word warrior with a high level of creativity. I have a vivid imagination and that imagination serves to bring me a balance between depth of insight and day-to-day reality. When I read a book, I see the story happening in my mind like a movie in cinemascope and technicolor. I have an ability with extrasensory perception which is much greater than that of the average person; a sensate, as the old terminology would call me. I feel and experience life so powerfully that often, being in the company of some people, is almost unbearable. Psychic and intuitive to the extreme, I feel life has been a challenge. For knowing what I know, and feeling the world so intensely, takes great strength of mind and a good firm hold on reality in order to maintain one's sanity.

Once again, I sat huddled at my computer, feeling the surge of energy flow through my whole being. This morning however, as the words began to flow, somewhere off in the distant corridors of my mind I could hear the voice of John Cleese from *Faulty Towers*. He was reading my manuscript and it was as though I was listening to a radio station. 'God, I'm really cracking up,' I mumbled as a smile crossed my face. So with great amusement, it was on that day that I had the realization that life really is like an episode of *Faulty Towers* and it never does turn out quite as you expect it to. Often when you look back in hindsight, all the drama and a great deal of the chaos were quite unnecessary and are all quite ridiculous.

I was still trying to get my heart past Mr. Charming and wondering why fate had dealt me such a cruel blow. There was nothing else for it but to knuckle down and throw myself 100 per cent into my work of writing and developing the Game of Life. But, without warning, my computer died and I had no money to buy a new one. My older sister (Bless her!), went out and bought a computer which she promptly gave to me to use. I will never forget that act of generosity and one day, I hope to be able to pay her back tenfold. Life was challenging, and in the midst of all this, there would be even more changes and adjustments for me to make.

Meanwhile, across town, Murray was struggling to keep his

courage and sanity as life without his wife was a very hard road. A new baby and a twelve-year-old daughter to look after, while working sixty hours a week, would have broken a lesser man; but not Murray. He just kept on moving on, being a dad, and finding ways to cope with what life had handed him. He never once complained. He dug deep within his body, mind, and soul and found the strength he needed for his children. There was no time to feel his own grief, that would have to wait; he just kept on moving on, making his way forward.

Although I was not able to do much, I kept watch over the fragile household of Murray and the children from a distance. I didn't want to interfere, and after all, Maori tradition is that family looks after its own. I grieved more than I had ever grieved in my life. I just could not understand how a woman I had known for only one year could touch my soul so deeply and open my heart to reveal the very core of my being. With Allana's passing, it was as though a part of me had died with her. Yet, life had to continue on; and would, in its bizarre way.

Our house at number 62 was now under constant surveillance. Men with cameras were sitting in cars as though to let us know we were being watched—scare tactics, and they were working! Our phone lines were being tapped and we were being monitored in every way. Occasionally, someone would enter the house. We knew when computers or anything else had been checked, but what could we do? Mysterious lights were shone through windows in the middle of the night. My sister had reached breaking point; her absolute distress was more than she could cope with. 'We'll all wake up dead one morning,' she exclaimed anxiously, 'I don't know how much more I can take of this.' To be honest, neither did I, or my personal assistant Lynne. The constant threats were about all a body could take.

My dreams led the way forward, my spirit visitors came and went as they usually did, and life was very much as it was in *Alice in Wonderland*. In spite of everything, I held onto the belief that I could achieve the impossible, and I did just that. The board game was becoming a reality inch by inch. Anything I wanted and worked towards just materialized. My instincts told me what to do, who to contact, and how to do exactly what I needed to do to reach my goals. While other people took the long road to get to where they wanted to go, my way was to cut straight to the chase. Talk to Richard Branson—well, why not! I was told he would not reply to my letters or my attempts to share my big picture. People were wrong! I thought of ways to get his attention and I did! He wrote me twenty or more letters, all short and to the point. However, I never did get to sit down and talk with him, not yet anyway! When the board game finally came off the printing press, the very first prototype was sent by courier straight to Richard Branson's London office. A week later, a letter came back congratulating me on my achievement, wishing me all the best, and saying he could not wait to play the game with his kids. I wonder if he ever did. Shortly after that, his life went into overdrive with the setting up of Virgin Blue, and Virgin Airlines in Australia. Bad timing for me! More letters transpired, but the important ones often mysteriously disappeared, turning up in the mail box six months after the posting date. It was like, as I pushed forward, there was someone or something trying to stop my progress. Was it Mr. Charming and his friends? Or, was it just the plain and simple fact I was ahead of my time?

Now, you may think my life until now had been complex, but hey, it was about to fly to a whole new level and undergo another impressive change of pace. We have all heard it said that in hindsight everyone has 20/20 vision. Would I have pushed on 'where angels feared to tread' if I had known then what I know now? Yes, probably. I have always had an altruistic attitude toward life and my path. I just always believed that if the energy was right, the money would appear to make it happen. I began this project with very little money; in my life money has always been my biggest challenge. My dream—well, it was 'big'! And I must admit, there were times when I questioned my own sanity as I pushed forward with ten dollars to my name. How on earth was I going to manifest enough money to complete this project? I had the deep conviction God would send me an angel; and guess what, He did just that.

From time to time, I would check in on Murray and the kids, never allowing myself to get too attached to playing mum. I felt I already had too much to do; and mostly, I didn't want to interfere. It saddened my heart to see how the man struggled to keep body, mind, and soul together. John Boy was already walking and this little blonde bombshell had a smile that I had no doubt would one day sink ships and launch rockets to the moon. Life moved on ….

Trying to create a million-dollar product with nothing more than willpower, seemed to be pure madness. I needed to have financial support and I needed people around me who had the same altruistic bent that I possessed. It wasn't just about the money. When finally the money was there, the biggest problem was that people who claimed to be experts, either knew less than I did, or didn't have any common sense. Everyone wanted to put their own spin on the product. Their limited view of how they perceived it, created a wall of issues, all of which I kept breaking down. I wasn't a person to buckle under the demands of others so, as usual, I just stood my ground. I supported myself by working back at the expos, life-coaching, and running training programs for corporate business and government.

Some days, dealing with life, as well as all the complexities of my vision, was like trying to give birth to a 20 kg baby. It took its toll on me financially, physically, and emotionally. Eventually, I understood that if this project was to happen, then I would be the only person who could do it. The frustrating part was that the knowledge of the project was all in my head. It was my vision, and most people didn't have the ability to even catch a glimpse of what I was trying to achieve. So I just kept on moving on, acting with precision, and trusting in God and my knowing to show me the way. I just kept taking one step at a time, forward into the unknown, without a parachute. The universe continually demanded more and more of me. The faster I understood something, the sooner another challenge would appear. It wasn't long before the stress and strain of it all began to show.

I could tell that my health was deteriorating; 30 August 1997 began with a migraine from hell which lasted for days. The doctor had been called more than once to give me an injection of Pentothal which he said would fix the problem. Apparently my condition was compounded by my previous illness; that, and pushing my body, mind and spirit to the limit. I had been sick on and off for so long and was now so ill, I just wanted to go to sleep and never wake up again. I just stayed in my room and slept for days and days. Eventually, little by little and step by painful step, I tried to put my life back together. But by now, Mum's health was declining rapidly. Age had finally caught hold of her in both hands. She was visibly getting thinner and thinner every day. We tried to lighten her mood by telling her she was the shrinking lady; God bless her, she had not been well for a very long time. Taking Mum's health into consideration and my own, plus the fact that I was financially in a difficult situation, I had no choice but to once again go back on sickness benefit and put most of my plans on hold. It was time to take time out, rest, heal, and look at the bigger picture of my life—where was it going and how the heck was I going to get from here to there?

At eighty-two years of age, I knew Mum was hanging on to life simply because she wanted to be sure all of her children would be all right. In those last months, Mum and I spent hours talking. For the first time in our lives, we were close, the way I always wanted it to be. My mother had lived a very complicated life. Marjorie Fisher Neale, born 8th April 1916. She was the daughter of Alice Emily Neale, a domestic who lived at 52A Trafalgar Street in Brighton, England. After extensive research, we found out that my mother was born in a private hospital for young unmarried women at 83 Sunderland Road in Forest Hill, England. Her mother had been working as a domestic at a house tended to by a Dr. Fisher Sr. One of his three sons was Dr. Frederick A. Fisher Jr., a man who was recognized by his hunched back, said to have been the result of being dropped by his nanny when he was a baby. Dr. Fisher Jr. was married to a mid-wife named Alice. They had no children themselves and so arrangements were made to foster my mother when she was born. In England, before adoption was legal, it was common for unmarried mothers to nominate the foster father as the father on a birth certificate, in order to give a child to another family. Everything was set in motion when Alice delivered the baby girl in the hospital.

In our talks together, Mum told me how she even went to the trouble of hiring a private detective to try to find her mother at the end of WWII. The result of that search was that she was informed her mother was a War Bride who had recently left England to go and live in Canada. Sadly, while alive, there were no answers found for my mother. She reassures me from the other side however, that they have now found each other and everything is fine.

During those last weeks of her life, Mum told me stories about her childhood and the horrors of living in the Barkley Buildings. She told me how her stepmother used to beat her and dress her in black stockings so the welfare workers couldn't see the bruises. The old lady, as Mum called her, was quite the bitter, nasty old lady—truth be told. My mother was not allowed to play with other children and she was constantly told, 'You are not like them. You cannot mix with the lower class.' Mum had no idea she was adopted until after the death of her stepmother. At that time, she found a total of sixteen birthday cards (one for every year), tucked away in a trunk in the attic. Granddad did the best he could, but not even he could protect Mum from the old lady's vengeance. A childhood of abuse, illness, and never much affection left its scars. Yet all in all, Mum was the best mother anyone could ever have wished for.

It was only a matter of time. My mother's tiny body was failing fast and no matter how stubborn and strong-willed she was, it was going to happen. Finally, on 19 June 1998 Mum passed away, leaving the family to deal with their grief. Her ashes were sent back to England where she was tucked away with the rest of the family next to Dad, Grandma, and my brother and sister in the family grave. It was the end of an era, both parents gone and the family, such as it was, left scattered to the four winds.

CHAPTER TEN

'Ask questions.'

The days spent living with my family at Number 62 can probably go down in history as some of the most challenging and difficult of days in the story of my board game's creation. I thought life was tough, but I had no idea that God still had more stripping to the bone for me just around the corner. He (God) was about to ask the most important question of all, 'Do you really believe in yourself and what are you doing? If you do, then prove it!'

I am sure I strained relationships to the max due to my stubborn fixation with getting this project completed. I have no doubt that at times I was unfair and irrational, and I know I hurt people who meant the world to me without realizing. Looking back, I can openly admit that I sure had a heck of a lot to learn. During this time, my spirit guardians kept visiting me in the early hours of the morning. They would take me on journeys to other places and other times, their intention being simply to trigger my memory and to set me on the ultimate path to healing my soul. With their guidance, my perceptual ability grew strong and fast. It was as though life was a constantly evolving scene; what appeared to be truth one day would no longer be appropriate for the circumstances the next.

Then in the very early hours one November morning, I had a special visitor. It was my old friend, my Aboriginal guardian; I woke from a deep sleep to see his smiling, dark face looking into my eyes. His hair jiggled and the tight curls danced in the light of the aura surrounding his head. He had not visited me in this way since I was a little girl so I knew something 'big' was happening. I was wide awake and I could see him there in the room. It wasn't a dream, this was real. I have to admit I was a little stunned as he reached his hand towards me and, with his index finger, touched the centre of my forehead. Just then, a flash of light so bright engulfed me. In an instant I knew my soul had once again taken flight, leaving the human form behind to rest quietly in a warm, safe bed. 'It is time,' he said as he waved his hand. In the passing of a second, I stood high on a mountain top, a sheer cliff below me. One gesture was all that transpired, 'This is our land, these are my people, and you have been chosen.' Even though he spoke in a tongue foreign to me in this life, I understood exactly what he was saying. How very strange this was. My mind flashed back to my childhood adventure at the Moodlu quarry and his visit to me there. What did he mean by, 'It is time.' and 'You have been chosen.'?

His voice was soft and yet a little husky as he spoke, so that I more than heard his words—I heard his heart. 'You are the first white one to pass our challenge. Your initiation has been long and hard, but you have stood the test of honesty and truth. Never before has this been achieved.' It was as though I was a part of everything he showed me that day, as my friend led me through the bush and along the top of the cliff face; showing me plants, seeds, animals, and spirit people. It seemed as though I had been there forever, so much time seemed to pass and I felt so at home. 'Now it is time,' he said. We want you to help heal this land and heal its people. This is what my people ask of you.' I had no idea what he meant, except that in some way I understood that I had the blessing of the Indigenous people of the land where I now lived. It felt quite humbling and in some ways totally overwhelming. In the months that followed Apari Orad's visit, I think I was visited by a head person from every Indigenous tribe in the world–African, Indian, Mexican, Spanish, Icelandic, and other spirit visitors trailed through our home like a constant caravan of faces and color. It came as a surprise to me to learn that I was not the only one to see these visitors. I never forget an Irish friend named Bridget who had come to stay the night at our home. The next morning, she woke up looking as if she had not slept at all. 'For f… sake, Lesley, what the hell is happening here? There was a procession going through my room all bloody night!' Bridget lamented in her strong Irish brogue. 'All bloody night they passed through saying 'hello'. What the hell! I ended up facing the wall. It was the only way I could get any sleep!' It was funny but true. Everyone saw them, it didn't matter whether they usually saw spirit or not. People found our house very fascinating indeed.

There must have been a reason they chose to honor me with their presence but all I could think was that I was just a simple country girl in a big city full of people who, it seemed, only wanted to get out of me what they could. How was it that so very few people really cared about the welfare of others and the unnecessary suffering in this world? My view was that it could all be stopped through providing the right tools for people to help themselves. That was the mindset that always motivated the work that I did. So I was determined to find a way to get the first board game developed and manufactured. I knew what it could do to help people, and I also knew that it was not going to be an easy task. After all, who would give a girl from the bush with no business credibility a go? All I had left to pull strength from was my sheer stubborn willpower and the vision of what I wanted to accomplish. Then one day, fate brought me to meet a wonderful man who became my very own unlikely angel. The gentleman who helped finance the initial stages of my board game's development requested that there be no mention of him, or his story in this book. So while I must respect his privacy, I remain forever in his debt; and grateful for his financial, physical, and emotional support. He even wanted to marry me, but I could not commit; and sadly, the stress of my venture and the financial burden was more than he could bear. We finally parted ways in 2002. Life moved on and once again I was cut adrift, left to flounder in a sea of uncertainty. At work there was also unease; the wolves were hammering at my door and everyone was ready to abandon ship, leaving me to die a thousand deaths emotionally.

Under my shaky guidance, my company entered into the manufacturing phase and the 'on the ground' trials of the board game, *TRUITY - The Game of Life*[11] had been launched. It was so confusing. I didn't want the product to be a physical box of things; I wanted it to be a computer product, but everyone dismissed the idea. Eventually, I caved into the pressure and manufactured five thousand games.

The real money wasting started with warehousing, fees, sales people … My vision went from one of incredible belief to one of total disaster. It's true that some lessons are hard learnt. My lesson was the simple fact that I should have done what I wanted and not

---

[11] TRUITY – The Game of Life (see Postscript)

listened to what other people told me I had to do. My journey into personal development was a blessing at this time in that it began to ease my suffering. I needed understanding and the only way to get that was to dive straight into my own situation. The more I understood of my own problems, the more I wanted to help other people not to live the same hell as I was living. It was my own and other people's suffering that led me to make the board game in the first place. I had seen needless emotional suffering everywhere in the workplace. Clients I had in the past just were not prepared for life and I honestly felt I could do something to help empower them. I also felt that I still had so far to go and so much to discover and achieve myself in the process of developing the board game. These were my incentives to keep going.

As fast as the money came in, it went out. There was always another idea, always another trademark, always more development, but never enough time. Finally in 1999, the first printing and manufacture of my board game was completed. Trials were arranged, and tests on the physiological effects were set in motion. The first step was to send the product out all over the world. People were invited to trial and test the board game in different settings and environments within different types of organizations and institutions. I know I could have set it all up more effectively. I could have followed up more than I did, and I probably could have approached the whole thing in a very different way to achieve a different outcome. The problem was that everyone who saw and used my product could see a different angle of how it could be applied. I had invented a super monster, one that went anywhere and could be adapted to address any question and any category and still work just as profoundly, regardless. One train of thought was that I should license it for corporations, as that was where the money was. Another train of thought was to use it in medical fields for depression and rehabilitation. I can be quite frank and honest about it all; there is nothing to be gained in hiding the reality of my adventure. The problem was, I knew what I wanted to do; I wanted to help common people. That is where my heart was, and I didn't ever do it for the money. Making a heap of money, to me was just a means to help more people.

Since I began developing the Game of Life, I had grown more as a person than I could ever have imagined. I had become strong, independent, and confident of my own worth and capabilities. Eventually, my product was being used in rehabilitation hospitals, corrective services, schools, and government departments across the world. No one really understood the magic behind how or why it worked, but they saw the power of what it could do to change people's lives, as well as the way they dealt with life challenges. The biggest problem was, I wanted it to help anyone and everyone, not just corporate people, or people with money. This fact made marketing almost impossible. I wasn't making any money from the game, and we actually had to give it away to get corporate and government to trial it. My biggest problem was, I had created something that institutions wanted validation for. Even though there was nothing but praise for the way the game transformed people's thinking and lives, the obstacle was that I didn't have ten years of empirical evidence. To add more pressure to the mix, I had discovered that a German man had tried to steal my *TRUITY* trade mark. He had registered a website and was starting a company in New Zealand where I legally owned the Trade Mark. What on earth was the world coming too! His comment when I confronted him was, 'Try to fight me, you will find I have very deep pockets.' The battle to survive had begun!

Psychologists heralded the product as pure genius. Psychiatrists said it was the modern day antidepressant. *TRUITY- the Game of Life* was called the revolutionary tool for improvement of human behavior and for the development of emotional intelligence. Everyone who reviewed the product wanted to make it complicated and that fact really frustrated me. I wanted to create something that people didn't have to be rocket scientists to use—something which could help normal, ordinary people learn to handle difficult life situations more easily. I didn't want corporate licenses and contracts, and people turning what I had created into a monster fix-it for the rich and famous. I had invented something so enormously life changing; but the truth was, I didn't have the money backing to get it where it needed to go.

CHAPTER ELEVEN

'Turn every obstacle into an opportunity.'

Charlemagne once told me, 'The greatest thing a person can ever achieve is the courage to be who they were born to be'. When I researched my family history, it revealed a strong family line of honest hard-working people. I discovered school teachers, sculptors, stone masons and soldiers. In the present generation, my mum took pride in teaching us solid British values–to have integrity, courage, and consideration; to be thoughtful and respectful, and to honor those around us. There was always love in our house; Mum and Dad were in love and happily married for forty-five years. The five surviving children of their marriage are all very different people. My sister is somewhat like me, but more into environmental conservation and permaculture. One brother became an engineer; another, a nurse; and one, a general laborer. I have just kept stretching boundaries all of my life by becoming a mum, a nurse, a therapist, a miner, an artist, an author, and an inventor. I'm always looking to develop something to help ease suffering.

The last ten years had seen my life change so dramatically that I felt as though it had moved into the fast lane. Everything, in both my personal and business life, was moving at one hundred miles an hour. Before I knew it, new corporate offices were opened in the main street of Brisbane. Here, lawyers were tying up my product in a million dollars worth of red tape, and graphic designers were turning my rough sketches into works of art right before my eyes. I had reached a place where I felt I had conquered my first mountains and I could measure the journey. I was confident enough financially to rent a small apartment in the city which overlooked the river. From there, I could sit and watch the world go by. Life was good! For the first time in many, many years I felt that I had entered the world where I belonged, the place of power and change. Everything I ever wanted was within my reach.

I was surprised to find I actually liked living in the city. It was exciting having everything at my fingertips (restaurants, movies, shopping) and not needing to drive miles in heavy traffic to get to work. If I needed some fresh air, I could walk down to the river, catch the City Cat, and just travel anywhere I wanted up and down the river. Or, I could walk to Southbank and sit having supper and a glass of wine while looking out at the lights, and without having to worry. There was no end to the magic, and no end to the workload in front of me. I became consumed by my vision, and it wasn't long before my soul was growing tired again. I longed for home, the beach, and peace to fill my life. I still had not found Henry the VIII, as Josie used to jokingly call him. My life was somewhat empty of the good stuff that makes the heart sing. I was giving more than I had, and since my angel investor and I had parted company, there was no corner of comfort. There was no one to boost my spirits and encourage me to keep going. My vision was so big, and my problem was that I was trying to do it with pennies. I needed someone to financially back further development of the board game to make it happen.

I had not seen Allana's family for quite a while and I felt I needed to honor my promise to her; I decided it was time to check in to see how Murray and the kids were going. All was as best it could be. Janine was still in school and she seemed to be growing up to be the normal rebellious teenager. John Boy had grown so much, and although it defied logic, he always seemed to recognize me, running straight into my arms with lots of hugs and kisses. I was in love but with a little boy with big brown eyes, blonde hair, and one heck of a cheeky smile. Small and cuddly would have to do. My heart felt as though we were connected by an invisible string of golden light. I felt so helpless to do anything to help Murray; all I could do was to be a friend and to listen.

It was time to consider closing the business down, shutting the offices, moving back home, and getting ready for the next stage of my adventure. But before I did so, I applied for venture capital to fund the next stage of development; I believed I could do it, that I could raise the finance for the second stage. Business plans were written and all those who could feed off of the business and my naive trusting approach gathered like bees to a honey pot. Even Mr. Charming talked me into paying him thousands of dollars to develop Serenity documents for my computer website. It is a horrible way to learn about business, to have your trust broken and your money devoured by unethical people. Everyone was an expert, but in reality, I could not find anyone who could actually deliver what they promised. Then, out of the abyss of financiers, one group stood up and asked to see my business plan and to conduct a viability study of my project. The glimmer of hope was still flickering.

At about the same time as the venture capitalist showed up, I was contacted by a major USA company which specialized in education. They wanted me to travel to Salt Lake City, Utah to introduce them to my board game. Everything looked so positive. We spoke at length of contracts and the opportunity for one of the biggest players globally to retail my product through their three hundred and twenty-one retail outlets. Trips to Salt Lake City were undertaken and the meetings went well. It looked as though everything was falling into place. Or, so I thought. Little did I know that the moment they found out I had run out of money, the walls came crashing down and all communication and negotiation came to a screeching halt. This was another deafening blow to my soul as another nail was pounded into the coffin of my beloved creation, *TRUITY.*

Before I knew it, months had passed and it was June 2002. It was a hard decision but I chose to close the Brisbane offices. Staff was laid off, and I think I was close to a breakdown by that time; everything stretched my nerves to shreds. I lost some very good friends over how things progressed. People had high expectations and, in truth, no one knew that behind the scenes I was trying to deal with the potential of a financial disaster which tore at my heart and soul. I moved home to Sandy Beach…leaving the life I had carved out of nothing behind me. I was tired, and although I still waited for the venture capitalists to finalize the details of our contract, I needed time out.

CHAPTER TWELVE

'Emotions turned inward create illness.'

The Brisbane offices were now closed. Sometimes I wondered if that interlude of business entrepreneurship in my life had ever happened at all. I felt my staff let me down, or did I let them down? I felt my generous nature had been taken advantage of. I had been used and abused by a whole range of people, including my attorneys, my staff, and a list too long to mention. Mr. Charming too, had somehow managed to play me like a fish by getting contracts to do work for me which delivered no substance at all to my business. I was angry with myself and there were just so many unanswered questions.

I was now back at Sandy Beach and trying to adjust to the change in lifestyle and the changes in my life. What had I done, run away again? Had I made the right choice? I had a life here once but that was a very different life. Even though I was married with children, I didn't have many friends. The friends I did have were like me—a bit zany, spiritual, and into healing and alternate health. Reality is, I didn't fit in here when I lived here before. What on earth made me think I would fit in now? I sat and watched the passing parade of faces, quite surprised that I could still recognize so many of the people as they passed by where I sat, and yet not one of them recognized me or acknowledged me. I had come home, but to what? I felt confused and embarrassed that I had set out with such grand plans and now I seemed to be hanging in mid air with no particular way to proceed.

So once again I decided to put myself out on a limb and, with the help of my local accountants, set out to get some much needed venture capital. I had been hanging on by a thread. Money was so tight and I had no real way forward except to sell a part of my venture. I needed to gain a foothold to get back into the market and finish the development. And, I wanted to take my idea to its real target. You see I never intended the board game to be a board game. My end vision was to have it as an Internet product—something anyone, anywhere in the world could use. I knew how to make it happen; I just didn't have the resources to make it happen. Finally, the venture capitalists put forth an offer which made me think that maybe, all was not lost. Contracts were delivered, product evaluations were completed, and all the preliminary paperwork was finalized. The venture capital company had offered to buy 42 per cent of my company for 1.5 million pounds and they had also offered to invest another 1.5 million pounds 'interest only' for seven years. I held my breath and prayed things would continue to move forward. There was no going back, that's for sure; I had burnt my bridges!

I had my accountants check out the venture capitalists, and they assured me everything was genuine. The scheduled signing was in sight, until a phone call early one morning from England. My hopes were taken from floor to ceiling and then back to the floor and underground when the venture capitalists decided to have a change in plans right at the last minute. They decided the money they were going to invest in my company would best be invested in oil due to the start of the Gulf War. I fell apart, big time! My confidence was shattered, my heart broken, and there was no one to talk through the devastation of what was happening.

I tried with all my heart to sort it out. My accountants were of no help; my lawyers offered even less assistance and my business friends, well … they all ran for cover. The only ones who stood by me were a few precious people. One long time friend, hearing of my situation, turned up at my door with the money to go to London and chase these rats. Another dear friend kept paying my car payments for me. And my best friend and PA, Lynne, continued to stand beside me no matter what went down. My life was in shattered pieces but there was no way I was about to give up on my dream, my vision of helping people in this world.

I learned some very harsh lessons that summer about business and the world of finance. I learned that things are never what they seem, and not everyone who claims to be ethical is actually ethical. My trip to London left me without resolution. The venture capitalists were nowhere to be found; they operated out of a virtual office space. I guess that works for them, as they are protected from having to face people whose lives they have destroyed. Even though I am British by birth, the London offices of Fair Trading would not assist me. I became an emotional basket case, constantly in tears and constantly thinking of how I could find a resolution to the horrific situation I was now faced with. There were no answers; there was no help. My life had been shattered into a million pieces and I had no idea how to fix it. Everything I had worked so hard to achieve was now gone. There was nothing left but to return home to Australia. I needed to talk to my accountants to see what could be done to pull myself out of the hole I had so elegantly dug for myself.

My accountants turned out to be of little support in my time of need. I had been left in a very bad situation. There was no money to keep paying them, and they just wanted to be paid so they could get me out of their hair. I guess they didn't understand the world of Intellectual Property any more than I did. Oh, they still charged big money; but looking back, the advice they gave was actually the one thing that ended my company and shattered my dreams. Their advice was to appoint an administrator, which I did. They advised me that if I went down this track, the intellectual property would remain with me, along with the remainder of the five thousand games and some cash in the bank. I trusted what they said, but at the end of the day, all I had left was my intellectual property; I lost everything as a result of following their advice. There was nothing I could do but to settle down in my tiny rented house in Sandy Beach and day after day, walk the beach searching my soul for understanding and for a way to pick up the pieces and move forward. I felt empty and alone. My family could not understand what I was going through. I was so ashamed that I had failed.

Once upon a time, I believed that I could make a difference—I believed I had a destiny. After much soul searching I couldn't help but feel that somewhere inside of me something was missing. It didn't matter how hard I tried, life was like pushing through molasses. Should it be this hard? There had to be something missing in the mix of my energy and my ability to find success. It wasn't the money. The money was just a manifestation of the energy mix. No, something was wrong, something was missing, and that something was the love and support of one good man who would accept me, warts and all. Knowing this, all I could do was to keep struggling

211

onward, developing myself as a person, learning all I could, and waiting for the man whose destiny it would be to help me manifest my vision. I wondered how soon that would be, as the winds of change felt strong.

This feeling seemed to be reconfirmed by the clarity of mind I was able to achieve in my living space at Sandy Beach and its surrounds; it was awesome to say the least. There was now an inner peace that moved with me, no matter where I travelled. It seemed to pervade my home, which one friend referred to as 'a house of peace, a sanctuary, its warmth and love encapsulating all who entered. This inner peace was only sometimes disturbed by an uncertainty—I still questioned, was the tapestry of my life complete? I very much doubted it.

Around this time, my dad (who had passed away in 1979) had been visiting me in spirit. I had an uneasy feeling that something extremely confronting was about to happen, and I knew I would have no control over events, or the ability to avoid or change them. Dad was my messenger; he always came in relation to gifts of money coming in, or matters concerning the children. On this particular night, as was typical, my dad came to talk to me in a dream. In the dream, he took my hand and led me to a roadside on a hill. There, I could see my red sedan smashed up against a telephone pole. I ran towards the brightly flashing ambulance lights, only to see my son James screaming in pain. He was thrashing about on a stretcher as the ambulance men tried to stabilize him. I was yelling, 'Don't leave me, James! You can't leave me. Please don't leave me!' And with that, I woke, covered in perspiration and a sense of dread sitting in the pit of my stomach. The next thing I knew, my dad was standing at the foot of my bed. He reached his hand out to me saying, 'Love, listen to me, he will be all right, trust me. He will get through this.' With that I woke up–gasping for breath, covered in lather of sweat, and with tears streaming down my face. I knew then that the accident would happen, and I knew there would be nothing I could do to prevent it.

On the Friday, I drove to Brisbane to spend the weekend with my friend Lynne. All the time I was driving, I had an uneasy feeling that something was up; but exactly what, I wasn't sure. I arrived at Lynne's apartment at about 7.30 pm. Within minutes, the phone rang. It was my daughter Marie, 'Mum, you have to come home. James has been in an accident, his car hit a telephone pole. And Mum, it's not looking good.' My blood ran cold. All I could think of was the precognitive dream I had in which Dad reassured me, 'He will be alright!' My God! No, not my son! I was tired, so tired. To drive back that night would be crazy. I could end up in the hospital too, I thought, as I tried to calm myself. I phoned the hospital in Coffs Harbour, only to confirm that yes, James was in critical condition. They couldn't tell me much at that point in time except that he had punctured lungs along with other internal injuries and they were trying to stabilize his condition. There was nothing I could do; I was 400 km away from home.

After an unsuccessful attempt to rest, I headed back out in the early hours of the morning. I wanted to get to the hospital as soon as possible so I drove without stopping. All the while, I kept hearing my dad's voice echoing in my head, 'Trust me. He will be alright.' James was only three years old when my dad passed away, but Dad always thought he was a pretty cool kid, a real boy! A toy hammer and saw went everywhere that James went. Toy Tonka trucks, dozers, and all other things boyish accompanied him. I guess Dad had been watching over him all this time; or at least, that was what I hoped would be the case. James had had a very challenging life so far; he had not always made the smartest decisions.

Five days later, it was obvious that our boy was dying right before our eyes. He had a chest drain and severe infections; nothing the doctors were doing seemed to be helping him on his road to recovery. His father and I came at the problem from different angles; but between us, we managed to get James transferred to the Sydney chest hospital. The hospital had James flown to Sydney that day and I followed by car. James went into surgery for what we thought would be a three-hour operation; eleven hours later, he came out minus two lobes of his lung. For the first time in over a week I felt some confidence in his chances of recovery and was able to sleep soundly. It took a long time, but eventually, James did recover fully from the car crash.

My dad was right; James did get a second chance at life. To be given a second chance was precious and it was something that, thank God, James grabbed with both hands and ran with. Everything happens for a reason; sometimes we see the reason and sometimes we don't. I came through the experience wiser for having had the journey. And I learned, beyond any doubt, that Dad does watch over James. I trusted my dad in life, and now in death he proved to me he was still a man of his word. Dad's words, 'He will be alright, trust me. He will get through this.' gave me the strength to get through the experience and they gave my son hope that he would recover in the moments when he really needed that reassurance.

Days passed quickly and before I knew it, July 2003 had arrived. I sat in my upstairs lounge room at Sandy Beach. My fingers were tapping at the computer keyboard with the sound of a CD ('What a Girl Wants') resounding throughout the house. This was followed by Frank Sinatra singing 'I've got you under my skin'. Well, wasn't that the truth! The words echoed out across the polished floors: 'I would sacrifice anything, come what might, for the sake of having you near.' In hindsight, what a life I have had! No one would ever believe most of it. And love–yes, I have had love, but it never seemed to stay. I have always felt that there was a special someone out there that I had to find. How to have a husband without having a husband is what I called it. I was married to Henry for twenty-five years. Following our divorce, there had been several engagements. Looking back, I'm sure they would have been absolute disasters, had I married any one of those men. Still, I had the strangest feeling that Mr. Right had already crossed my path—not once, not twice, but in fact many times. It remained a mystery to me as to why I had failed to see or recognize him. The yearning deep inside me to be with someone who would accept me and love me unconditionally just would not go away. And, contrary to what anyone might have thought, I wasn't lonely. It was never that way. It was more like I had a future husband somewhere I was trying to find but I had left him in a bus station and couldn't remember which one.

At that moment I sat alone in my home feeling as though life had totally forsaken me. Why had I had such a difficult life? I had always tried to do the right thing, and I only wanted to help other people. Had I got it all wrong? Was the world I had stepped into looking for answers been the wrong direction to take? So many questions, but most of all had I missed my opportunity for love. Had the ship sailed without me? My mum always said I was too fussy for my own good and maybe that was the problem. I don't know. It seemed as though I had spent most of my time searching for someone who had integrity and the capacity to be honest; who was a gentle, yet courageous soul; and someone who loved me as passionately and as truly as I loved him. I wanted a relationship with someone I could trust—someone I could trust with all my heart and soul; someone who would not reject me, but would protect me and accept me for who I was and what I stood for.

I never wanted someone to take care of me. I am far too fiercely independent for that. I just wanted someone who had their own life to live, yet was willing to stand behind me, yelling from the sidelines, 'Come on, girl, you can do it.' I imagined him to have a sense of humor that bordered on the ridiculous and a depth of integrity, vision, and passion that matched my own. I imagined that his love would take me to another world beyond the physical. I longed for that world where time and space no longer existed—a world where I no longer searched and a world where there was peace in my heart. Yes, I was guilty of searching for someone who would complement me. I was guilty of searching for someone who would reflect my strength and above all, who would have the ability to love me without smothering me.

The CD clicked onto the next track of the song. Music certainly had the ability to bring memories flooding back and at the same time to provoke thinking about the future. He's got to be out there somewhere, I thought. I am fast approaching the big five. Oh hell, I never thought it would take this long to find him. I suppose if you think about it though, it had taken me this long to stand in my own personal power and to know who I was and what I stood for. I tried to reassure myself that if I had met Mr. Right before, I probably would have stuffed it up. I sure was a different girl today than I had been in years gone by. At this point in time I was still wondering how my journey would eventually come together. All I could do was to focus on the *now* and just keep moving on. I sought reassurance by reminding myself of the words of a wise old lady I knew who would simply say, 'What's meant for you, dear, won't go by you!' In this case, I sure hoped she was right. As it turned out, the love of my life was to be the most unlikely candidate of all.

I didn't see it coming. There were no signs. Life was so confusing—all of my knowledge, all of my following spirit and my heart consciousness seemed only to be causing me more and more destruction. It was as though God himself was determined to strip everything physical away from me. My company was no longer, and on top of that, the German who had jumped my trade mark was causing all hell to break loose. I was tired and my family had all but abandoned me. My big brother demanded that I give up the *TRUITY* struggle before he would speak to me again. How could everyone not see that this was what I was born to do! I felt desperate and alone. It was only a few very good friends who stood by me and tried to support me financially and emotionally.

I spent my days waiting for a sign, walking the beach, and just trying to find some peace inside of me. Living near the sea was good for the soul but I needed so desperately to move on. So I called to God for a sign and it came. Late one night about 2 am, my dear friend came to give me the message I waited upon. Allana appeared, standing in the doorway to my room. There was a ruby red, beaded curtain behind her and I remember thinking, gee that's pretty! 'You must find Murray, Les. You have to find Murray.' That's all she said and then she disappeared. How on earth was I going to find Murray? Next morning, bright and early, I could not get the message out of my mind. I had to find Murray. Now, where would I find him? I hadn't seen him for years. John must be six or seven by now. And I think I remember hearing that Murray had met a lady and was in a relationship. Well, I may as well phone the hotel he used to run, maybe he is still there, I thought. I rang the number and Andrew, an old friend of Murray's answered, 'No, Murray doesn't work here anymore, but I can give you his number. Hang on and I'll get it for you.' With that, I wrote down the number. Then I took a deep breath and dialed it. A familiar voice answered the phone, 'Runcorn Hotel. How can I help you?'

'Murray, is that you? It's Les.' My voice was shaking.

He answered, 'Les, how the hell are you? You are not going to believe this; I'm sitting here with your old business card in my hand wondering if you still have the same phone number. I had a dream last night and Allana told me I had to find you.' My mouth dropped open and I told him about Allana visiting me too. 'Well we'd better catch up,' he said. We arranged to meet a few days later, neither of us having a clue what was on the cards.

It was early morning. I had parked the car at Stones Corner and waited at the coffee shop where we had arranged to have breakfast and catch up. Next thing, this pair of arms threw themselves around my neck and all I could do was hug my little boy. He had grown so much but was a tad skinny, that's for sure. I looked up to see that familiar face smiling at me, just like always. 'How are you going girl?' he asked. And that is how it began. An hour later when we left the coffee shop, John was pushed his way between us, hugging us both. I took his hand in mine and Murray took my other hand in his. Then Murray turned to me and said, 'Well girl, I think we are supposed to be together; that's what the signs are telling us.'

I looked at him and said, 'You know, I think you're right.' And we walked forward together, hand in hand, with John smiling brightly between us. We were where we should be.

CHAPTER THIRTEEN

'Thoughts create prisons and freedom'

Love had come back into my life, not through the door I
thought it would; but in fact, the way it was always meant to be. For
a few years, I became a normal mum again—doing the dishes,
cooking meals, and driving John to school. God had seen to give me
a rest, and a blessing, in providing me with the most amazing family
anyone could wish for. This brief period was then followed by years
which have been somewhat difficult, to say the least. But I never gave
up my work of helping as many people as I could, in ways which
would steady them and heal them to continue their journey.

On the night of Boxing Day 2009 once again I was woken from
a deep sleep by a visit from Allana's spirit. She looked as she did all
those years ago, with healthy thick, black curly hair and glasses
perched on her nose. She looked so serious, 'How long have you had
that?' she said as she pointed to my chest.

'Had what?' I asked.

'The breast cancer,' she said.

'I don't have breast cancer,' was my response.

'Yes you do, and you get to the hospital fast!' was her reply.

On 5 January 2010 I lay on the operating table, in my thoughts, thanking my friend who had now, not only saved my sanity, but also my life. And life went on ...

Murray turned out to be the love of my life after all. To this day, we still joke that Henry VIII has come home, and as long as he does not cut off my head (again) in this life, everything will be alright.

POSTSCRIPT

In 1994 the board game TRUITY was created. The concept was designed to speed up the natural evolution of consciousness. While playing the game, new neural pathways are created as a result of combining the participant's own life experiences with the hidden formula built into the game components. The game incorporates moral and ethical decision making in a revolutionary new way which develops emotional intelligence. Three years of trialing the board game proved that it worked and did facilitate positive and permanent changes in thinking.

The product was never intended to be produced as a physical board game; a next stage was all lined up, ready to be set in motion. My vision is a system where the product would be available online for anyone, anywhere in the world to use. Sadly however, the financing fell through and I have not had the energy to make another run at my final goal. It will happen! How do I know this? Because it is my destiny to achieve this goal! This is how I will bring my gift to the table. This is how I will help thousands of people all over the world. The Lord spoke to me and I heard his voice. Miracles happen every day ... in my world!

The board game currently is not in production but is awaiting second stage funding to further develop the concept.

The game's applications and versatility astounded those who were involved in the first trials of the product. It currently remains in use in Corrective Services at Wacol men's and women's prison in Brisbane, Australia and in other training facilities. In addition, it is in use in hospitals, schools and over four thousand homes around the country. The TRUITY product cannot be used for monetary gain or in commercial environments without prior license being obtained from me, the owner. I still wait for a sign of how I can bring my vision to life–the TRUITY board game sits under the bed in the spare room.

Today, I live with Murray and John in our home in Northern New South Wales, not far from where I lived all those years ago, and close to my other children and grandchildren. My life has been an amazing adventure, more than I could write in one book. My days are filled with being an author and an artist; and of course, I help anyone who crosses my path and asks for help.

My skills are very unconventional. I am able to read the body's energy and diagnose issues that medical practitioners have missed. I see not only the future, but also the past. However, all of these skills are not what life is about. It is time people returned to basics, the basics of energy and life. Many who have jumped on the spiritual path have never learnt the most important skills of all. They seem to be more interested in the magic, rather than in the true mystery which surrounds everyday life.

Ultimately I now know and understand that walking a spiritual path will not necessarily provide you the answers. It will take you on journeys you need not take, and often cost you more than it gives back. The real answer does not involve spirits or psychic, it lies in your heart. We learn from the principles that

Jesus Christ himself taught. 'Love thy neighbor as thy self.' And it is that simple.

Life is really about doing a million small acts of kindness; from that, you truly can change the world!

Be kind to each other and mostly to yourself.

Lesley K Halverson
2014

www.ingramcontent.com/pod-product-compliance
Lightning Source LLC
Chambersburg PA
CBHW060919040426
42445CB00011B/704